The American Sign Language Handshape Puzzle Book

LINDA LASCELLE HILLEBRAND

Based on
The American Sign Language Handshape Dictionary
by Richard A. Tennant and Marianne Gluszak Brown

Illustrated by
Valerie Nelson-Metlay

Clerc Books
Gallaudet University Press
Washington, D.C.

Gallaudet University Press
Washington, DC 20002

http://gupress.gallaudet.edu

All sign illustrations and definitions for the puzzles and exercises in this book
can be found in *The American Sign Language Handshape Dictionary*
(Washington, DC: Gallaudet University Press, 1998).

ISBN 1-56368-310-5

This book is dedicated to our friends:
Doris and Arthur Nyquist, Helen Dalton, Kathy
(Grandma) and David Leonard, Kathy and John Murphy,
Rosemarie Fresh, Virginia Baumann, Ramona and Albert
Arneson, June and Albert Parish, Gary Schleicher, Lynda
Orne, and Karen Smith. These friends welcomed me and
my husband Tim into their families and their world and
taught us so much about acceptance, trust, humor, and
love. They taught us a little sign language, too!
We will never be able to repay them.

Contents

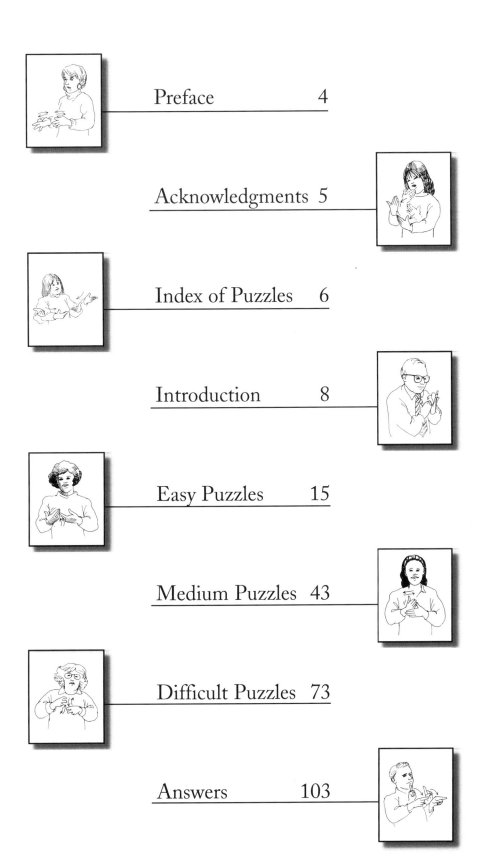

Preface

The American Sign Language Handshape Puzzle Book provides a variety of puzzles to help you learn, strengthen, or review your signing vocabulary. It was created as a companion to *The American Sign Language Handshape Dictionary* by Richard A. Tennant and Marianne Gluszak Brown. The puzzles are games, not tests, so feel free to use the dictionary whenever you are stuck on a sign.

Whether you are a new sign language student or have been signing for a long time, you will find puzzles to reinforce your knowledge of American Sign Language. The puzzles are divided into three difficulty levels—easy, medium, and difficult. Within each level, there are seven different kinds of puzzles—crossword puzzles, handshape order puzzles, matching games, word search puzzles, which one doesn't belong? puzzles, and sign description puzzles. Try them all! Sometimes the easy ones will provide the break you need; other times you will be looking for the challenge of a difficult puzzle. The answers to all the puzzles are located at the back of the book.

So, the next time you are waiting at the doctor's or dentist's office, or are riding in a car, bus, train, or airplane, or you just want to take some time for yourself, do some puzzles. Not only are they instructive, they are fun!

Acknowledgments

Anyone who has ever undertaken a project knows that the cooperation and help of many other people is an essential ingredient to success. This book would have never gotten off the ground had it not been for trust. That trust came from Richard Tennant and Marianne Gluszak Brown—two extremely talented authors who trusted me with their names and their unique dictionary, *The American Sign Language Handshape Dictionary*. I thank both of them. A special thanks to Richard Tennant for his suggestions and improvements to the text of this book. I wish their dictionary had been available when I began learning sign language.

Many thanks to Ivey Pittle Wallace and to Gallaudet University Press for their trust and willingness to work with someone they didn't know. As my editor, Ivey Pittle Wallace promptly returned every call or e-mail with help and guidance. She is very professional and reliable, and it has been my pleasure to work with her.

I would be remiss if I did not thank my friend, Lottie L. Riekehof, and Gospel Publishing for giving me a start. Lottie Riekehof's book, *The Joy of Signing*, was my textbook, and creating puzzle books for her book taught me so much more than sign. Thank you, Lottie.

My gratitude to the Deaf community knows no bounds. My husband Tim and I have been welcomed into the Deaf world from the first day we met Deaf adults. Who could have known that when I entered Helen Dalton's class, a wonderful, new world would open to us? Thank you!

Without a doubt, Craig Gullicksen has been my guardian angel from the beginning. Craig's knowledge of computers is amazing, and it is surpassed only by his patience and sense of humor. My numerous calls for help were never ignored. I thank Craig and his wife Kathy for their willingness to help me and for not changing their phone number.

I also want to thank my friend Tom Hillebrand. I can't remember a visit or phone call that did not include inquiries on the progress of this book. He always makes me feel that my work is important. I am so lucky to have his support and encouragement.

Last, but not least, I send my love and gratitude to my husband Tim. He willingly took a back seat so that I could work on this project. He has survived on more fast food than most kids ever dream of! His support and encouragement began long before this project started, and I know I can depend on it long after this book is completed.

Index of Puzzles

Introduction

All of the puzzles in *The American Sign Language Handshape Puzzle Book* are based on the signs in *The American Sign Language Handshape Dictionary*. The signs, their English meaning (gloss), and their descriptions are used as the puzzle clues. In order to solve the puzzles, you will have to look at a sign and write its gloss, match signs and glosses, and read descriptions and write the gloss.

The American Sign Language Handshape Dictionary is divided into two sections: one-hand signs and two-hand signs. Within each section, the signs are presented according to the handshape used to form the first part of the sign. The handshapes are based on the letters of the manual alphabet and the manual numbers, as well as variations of these shapes. The signs appear in a nearly alphabetical and numerical arrangement of the handshapes, as shown in the chart on page 9.

Sometimes the hands change shape during the execution of a sign. For example, the sign ADOPT* begins with the 5 handshape and ends with the S handshape. When the hands change shape, an arrow separates the two shapes and a colon separates the two hands, so ADOPT is written as 5 > S : 5 > S. In this sign, both hands have the same shape, but sometimes the hands assume different shapes. When this happens, the two handshapes are again separated by a colon. For the sign KEY, the hands are two different handshapes, X : Open B.

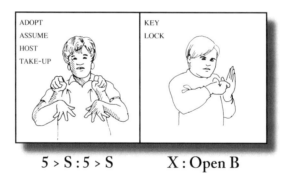

5 > S : 5 > S   X : Open B

Many of the puzzles require you to know the basic components, or *parameters*, of the signs. These parameters are handshape, palm orientation, location, movement, and nonmanual features or signals.

- **palm orientation** refers to the direction in which the hand is turned, such as palm up, palm down, palm left, etc.
- **location** refers to where the sign begins, such as near the forehead, below the eye, on the chest, etc.
- **movement** refers to how the hand (or hands) moves during the sign, such as arc hand forward, move hands down, etc.

The directions for each puzzle explain which parameter is used in that particular puzzle. Remember, these are puzzles, not tests. If you can't remember a sign or its meaning, look it up in *The American Sign Language Handshape Dictionary*. Each sign in the dictionary includes all of its parameters plus a description of how to make the sign.

* The English meaning, or gloss, of a sign is written in small capital letters.

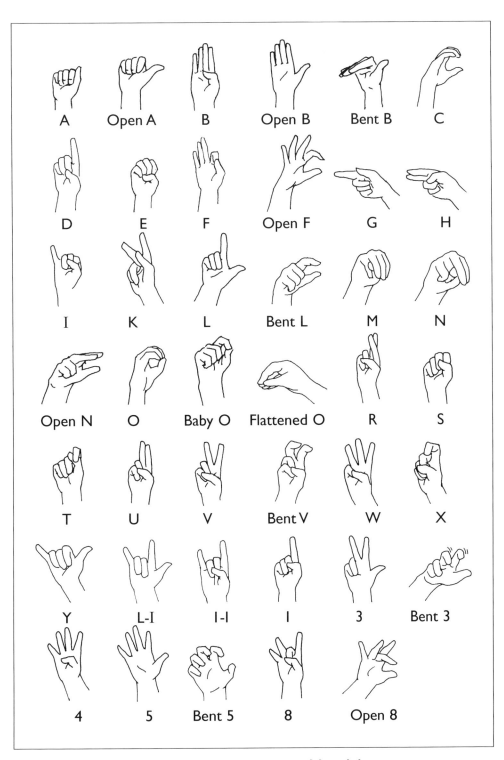

American Sign Language Handshapes

Types of Puzzles

Crossword Puzzles

These puzzles are just like other crossword puzzles, with one exception—the clues in the puzzles are signs rather than words. You will have to look at the sign and then write the appropriate gloss (English meaning) in the puzzle grid. The easy puzzles have as few as 6 signs, while the difficult puzzles have as many as 30 signs.

ACROSS

DOWN

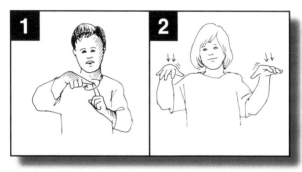

Multiple-Meaning Crossword Puzzles

The signs of American Sign Language represent concepts rather than single English words. Therefore, a sign can be translated into several English synonyms. For example, the sign CHOOSE can be translated as "pick," "choose," "select," or "appoint." In *The American Sign Language Handshape Dictionary* you will find from one to nine English words or phrases for a single sign. The context of the sentence determines which English gloss to use. The signs shown in the Multiple-Meaning Crossword puzzles have at least two glosses for you to write in the puzzle grid.

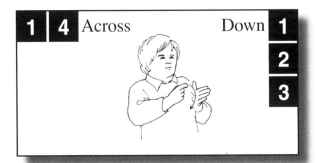

Handshape Order Puzzles

The purpose of these puzzles is to reinforce how important handshapes are in American Sign Language (ASL). Two signs can have the same location, palm orientation, and movement and differ only in handshape, but this difference changes the meaning of the sign. For example, the signs KNOW and THINK differ only in handshape. In the handshape order puzzles, you will see 14 different signs (see the example below). You must identify the handshape used in each sign and then number these signs in the same order you would find them in *The American Sign Language Handshape Dictionary*. You may also have to provide the English gloss for each sign. Check the handshape chart on page 9 or refer to the dictionary if you need help.

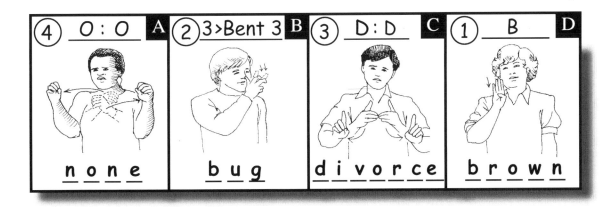

Matching Puzzles

The matching puzzles contain anywhere from 12 to 20 signs and a list of glosses. All you have to do is match the glosses to the correct signs. Sometimes there are more glosses than signs because a sign can be translated into more than one English word. There are answer spaces for each gloss. I have to thank my husband Tim for creating these puzzles.

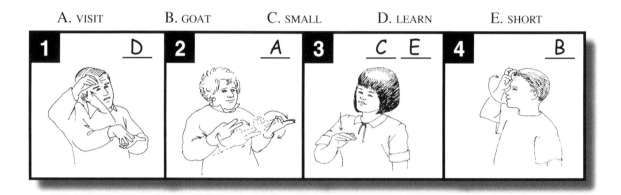

A. VISIT   B. GOAT   C. SMALL   D. LEARN   E. SHORT

Word Search Puzzles

Word Search puzzles are popular with people of all ages. The only difference between the puzzles in this book and puzzles in other books is that the clues here are signs rather than words.

Guess each sign and then look for its gloss in the puzzle grid. The glosses are written horizontally, vertically, and diagonally. Sometimes the letters read left to right and sometimes right to left. The easy puzzles have 16 signs, the medium puzzles have 20 signs, and the difficult puzzles have 24 signs.

1 LETTER

2 SISTER

3 HORSE

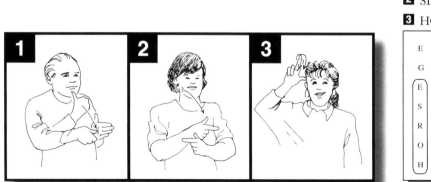

Which One Doesn't Belong Puzzles

For these puzzles, you need to find the one gloss in a list that doesn't belong with the other glosses. The clue may be about handshape, palm orientation, location (see the following example), or movement. Find the gloss that doesn't belong and write its corresponding letter inside the circle.

Ⓓ 1	Ⓑ 2	Ⓐ 3
A. HELLO	A. CAMERA	A. GAMBLE
B. BLACK	B. SUNSHINE	B. CELEBRATE
C. ROOSTER	C. BLIND	C. SNOW
D. ANALYZE	D. WAKE-UP	D. EXCELLENT
forehead	near eyes	above shoulders

Sign Description Puzzles

These puzzles show you how important it is to form a picture in your mind when thinking about a sign. The parameters—handshape, orientation, location, and movement—will be your clues. Each puzzle contains a list of sign descriptions. Read each description and try to make each sign. Write the gloss for the sign in the blanks next to the description. If you cannot guess the sign, just turn the page to find the sign illustration.

S • palm left • chest • bounce hand off chest twice   <u>c o u g h</u>

Sentence-Building Puzzles

Once you have developed a sizable sign language vocabulary, you can begin to combine signs into sentences. ASL has a different grammatical structure than English, so you must also learn the correct order for putting signs together. In the Sentence-Building puzzles, you will see a string of signs. First, write the English gloss for each sign inside its box; the number of blanks will tell you how many letters there are in each gloss. Then, look at the English sentences below the signs, and write the sentences again in ASL sentence order.

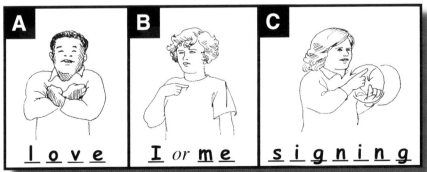

A <u>l o v e</u>   B <u>I</u> or <u>m e</u>   C <u>s i g n i n g</u>

<u>signing</u> <u>me</u> <u>love</u>
I love signing.

EASY PUZZLES

E1 Crossword Puzzle

ACROSS

DOWN

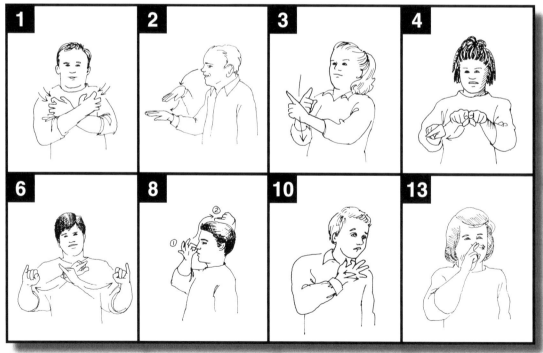

E1 Crossword Puzzle

The signs on the opposite page are for animals or words related to animals.
Look at each sign and write its English meaning in the spaces below.

E2 Handshape Order

Identify the handshape used in each sign and write it on the line above the sign. Then, number the signs in the same order you would find them in *The American Sign Language Handshape Dictionary*. Write the numbers 1–14 in the circles. If you need help, look at the handshape chart on page 9, or in the dictionary. Remember, the one-hand signs come before the two-hand signs.

○ ____ **A**

RAIN

○ ____ **B**

HOW

○ ____ **C**

TALK

○ ____ **D**

DUCK

○ ____ **E**

ANY

○ ____ **F**

TRY

○ ____ **G**

APPLE

○ ____ **H**

LUCKY

○ ____ **I**

I-LOVE-YOU

○ ____ **J**

GUITAR

○ ____ **K**

BROTHER

○ ____ **L**

SATURDAY

○ ____ **M**

CAT

○ ____ **N**

DINNER

E3 Matching

All of the signs below begin on the chest. Match the glosses with their signs and write the letter or letters on the corresponding lines. Remember, a sign can have more than one English gloss.

A. TIRED
B. POLICE
C. GRACIOUS
D. INTERESTING
E. EXHALE
F. DRESS

G. YOUNG
H. LIKE
I. EXHAUSTED
J. PRIDE
K. COUGH
L. GOWN

M. KIND
N. WE
O. BLOUSE
P. BREATHE
Q. US
R. PROUD

E4 Crossword Puzzle

ACROSS

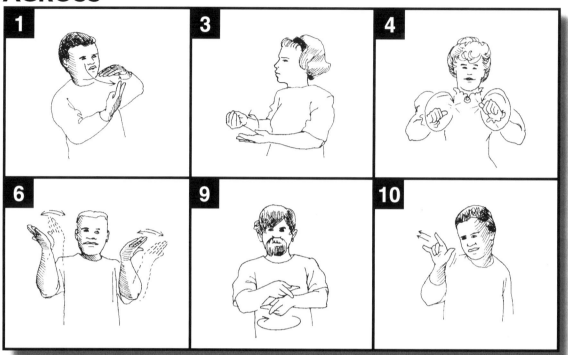

DOWN

E4 Crossword Puzzle

When you add the agent marker to each of the signs on the opposite page, you create the sign for a person who performs the action depicted in the sign. For example, TEACH + agent marker = TEACHER. Look at each sign, add the agent marker, and write the resulting gloss in the spaces below.

agent marker

E5 Crossword Puzzle

ACROSS

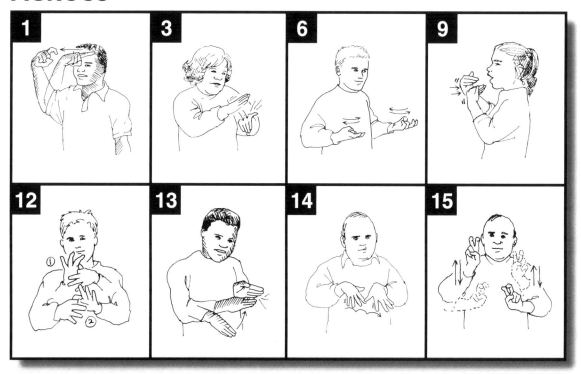

DOWN

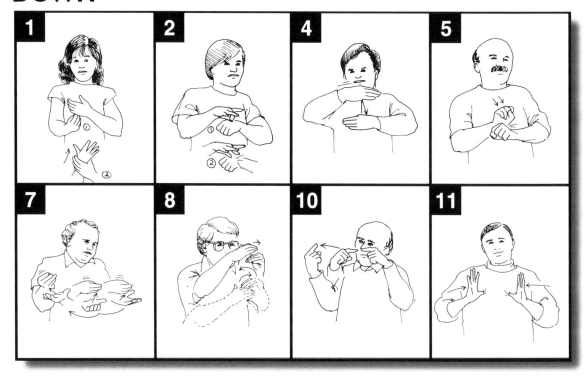

E5 Crossword Puzzle

The signs on the opposite page are related to warm weather activities. Look at each sign and write its English meaning in the spaces below.

E6 Word Search

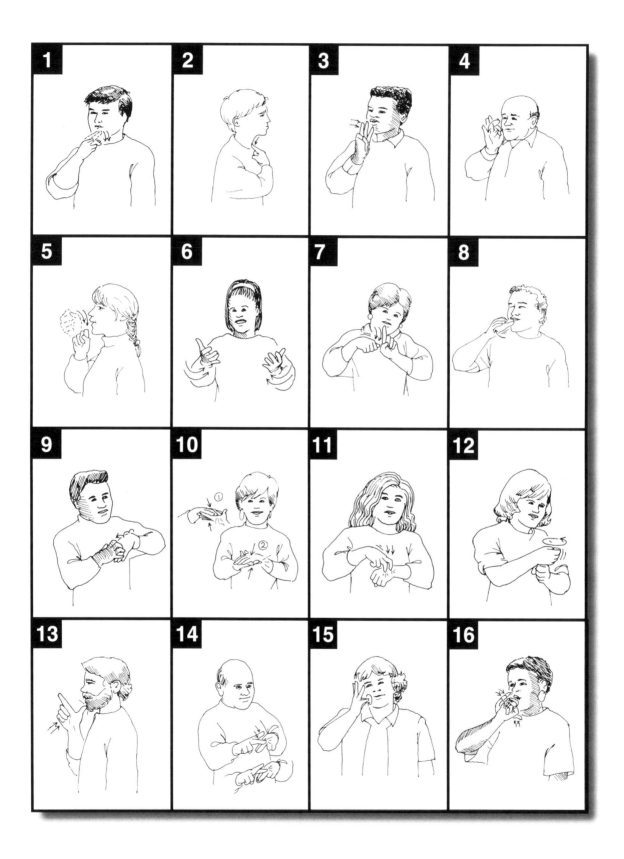

E6 Word Search

Each sign on the opposite page is related to food. Identify each sign and circle its gloss in the puzzle grid. The glosses are written horizontally, vertically, and diagonally. The letters may read forwards or backwards.

F	N	W	E	T	R	A	N	A	N	A	B	A
U	R	P	C	E	E	B	N	W	K	V	O	B
F	I	U	B	I	F	G	E	C	V	S	N	Y
M	C	M	I	N	H	F	N	T	C	M	T	E
L	E	R	L	T	Y	O	S	A	D	S	A	C
Y	C	A	G	R	A	P	E	S	R	D	L	E
T	R	S	I	K	N	R	C	I	D	O	T	J
H	E	J	L	C	F	L	H	F	F	E	E	D
G	A	F	S	W	A	T	E	R	J	P	R	O
V	M	M	E	S	I	Y	C	U	S	I	S	D
H	V	I	B	Y	P	N	T	W	N	B	O	G
C	H	R	E	U	F	S	E	K	A	V	T	W
N	K	A	M	B	R	E	L	M	G	H	A	K
U	P	H	D	S	E	G	O	W	N	I	T	O
L	O	R	U	A	L	N	E	E	F	F	O	C
V	D	G	T	L	G	A	T	R	H	I	P	Y
B	A	W	P	A	K	R	W	F	G	M	U	P
R	L	U	B	D	O	D	H	S	A	L	T	H

E7 Which One Doesn't Belong?

All but one gloss in each box represents a sign that is made palm or palms in. Determine which gloss does not belong in each list and write the letter next to the gloss inside the circle.

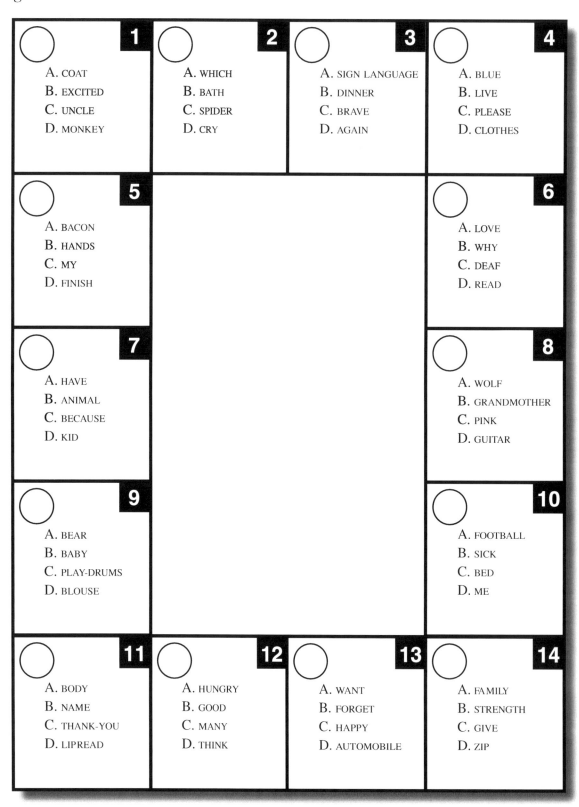

1
- A. COAT
- B. EXCITED
- C. UNCLE
- D. MONKEY

2
- A. WHICH
- B. BATH
- C. SPIDER
- D. CRY

3
- A. SIGN LANGUAGE
- B. DINNER
- C. BRAVE
- D. AGAIN

4
- A. BLUE
- B. LIVE
- C. PLEASE
- D. CLOTHES

5
- A. BACON
- B. HANDS
- C. MY
- D. FINISH

6
- A. LOVE
- B. WHY
- C. DEAF
- D. READ

7
- A. HAVE
- B. ANIMAL
- C. BECAUSE
- D. KID

8
- A. WOLF
- B. GRANDMOTHER
- C. PINK
- D. GUITAR

9
- A. BEAR
- B. BABY
- C. PLAY-DRUMS
- D. BLOUSE

10
- A. FOOTBALL
- B. SICK
- C. BED
- D. ME

11
- A. BODY
- B. NAME
- C. THANK-YOU
- D. LIPREAD

12
- A. HUNGRY
- B. GOOD
- C. MANY
- D. THINK

13
- A. WANT
- B. FORGET
- C. HAPPY
- D. AUTOMOBILE

14
- A. FAMILY
- B. STRENGTH
- C. GIVE
- D. ZIP

E8 Matching

All of the signs below begin on the nose. Match the glosses with their signs and write the letter or letters on the corresponding lines. Remember, a sign can have more than one English gloss.

A. FUNNY

B. FASCINATE

C. LOUSY

D. SKUNK

E. DON'T-CARE

F. BUG

G. FOX

H. HUMOROUS

I. MEDDLE

J. RAT

K. COLD

L. PRY

M. NOSY

N. MOUSE

O. DON'T-MIND

P. FUN

Q. AMUSING

R. INSECT

E9 Multiple-Meaning Crossword

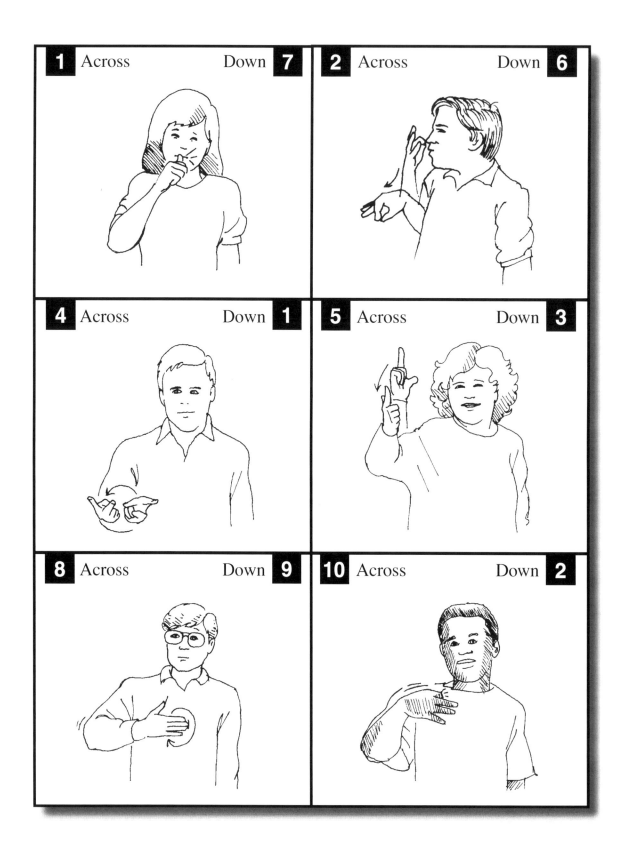

E9 Multiple-Meaning Crossword

A sign can be translated into more than one English word or phrase. Look at the signs on the opposite page; each sign has an "across" and a "down" answer. Write your answers in the spaces below. Good luck!

E10 Matching

All of the signs below can be associated with school. Match the glosses with their signs and write the letter or letters on the corresponding lines. Remember, a sign can have more than one English gloss.

A. HISTORY
B. ABSENT
C. SPELL
D. LEARN
E. MAINSTREAM
F. TABLE

G. SIT
H. DATE
I. CHEAT
J. STUDY
K. WHISPER
L. ALPHABET

M. TARDY
N. FINGERSPELL
O. DESK
P. SKIP CLASS
Q. BE-SEATED
R. LATE

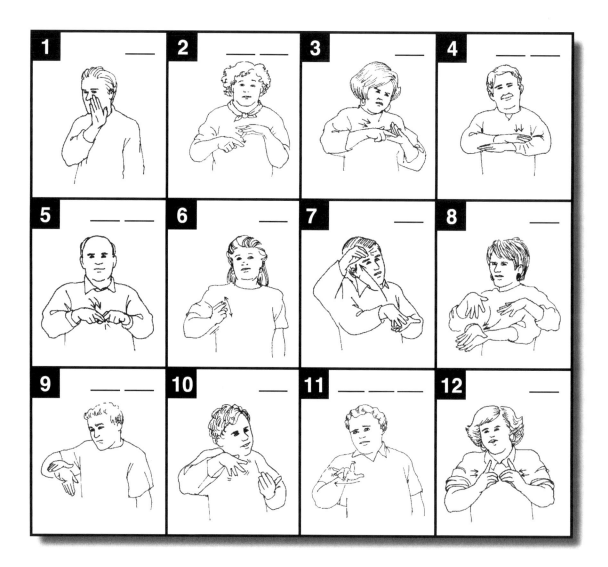

E11 Which One Doesn't Belong?

All but one gloss in each box represents a sign that begins with the handshape written at the bottom of the box. Determine which gloss does not belong in each list and write the letter next to the gloss inside the circle.

1
- A. BEARD
- B. SUN
- C. COMPUTER
- D. COMPLAIN
- E. CANADIAN

C

2
- A. VOICE
- B. BITE
- C. SEE
- D. STUCK
- E. SMOKE

V

3
- A. PLAY-CARDS
- B. SALAD
- C. BALL
- D. SPIDER
- E. AUDIENCE

Bent 5 : Bent 5

4
- A. DEPRESSED
- B. EXCITED
- C. COMPUTER
- D. DANGER
- E. SICK

Open 8 : Open 8

5
- A. RELAY
- B. DOUGHNUT
- C. RUNAWAY
- D. ROOM
- E. REPORT

R : R

6
- A. LEFT
- B. HAIR-DRYER
- C. LIE
- D. LUNCH
- E. LAZY

L

7
- A. LOUSY
- B. BOY-SCOUT
- C. VEHICLE
- D. DEVIL
- E. ROOSTER

3

8
- A. WORSEN
- B. ALL-NIGHT
- C. TABLE
- D. MUSIC
- E. NOTHING

Open B : Passive

9
- A. OLYMPICS
- B. IMPORTANT
- C. POSTPONE
- D. FLEXIBLE
- E. FAMILY

F : F

10
- A. STRUGGLE
- B. STRETCH
- C. COLD
- D. DEFEND
- E. COFFEE

S : S

11
- A. LIGHT
- B. EAGLE
- C. ONION
- D. NEED
- E. DETECTIVE

X

12
- A. HANUKKAH
- B. WAR
- C. LINE-UP
- D. TWINE
- E. PRISON

4 : 4

13
- A. ZERO
- B. OPINION
- C. WHO
- D. NONE
- E. PERCENT

O

14
- A. ME
- B. PRIVACY
- C. RED
- D. DEAF
- E. ALWAYS

1

E12 Multiple-Meaning Crossword

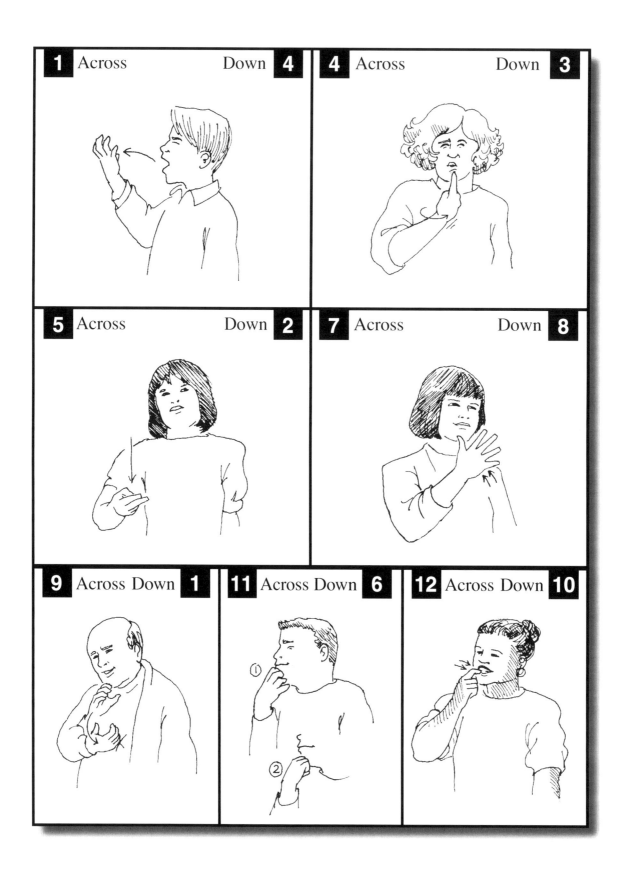

E12 Multiple-Meaning Crossword

A sign can be translated into more than one English word or phrase. Look at the signs on the opposite page; each sign has an "across" and a "down" answer. Write your answers in the spaces below. Good luck!

E13 Word Search

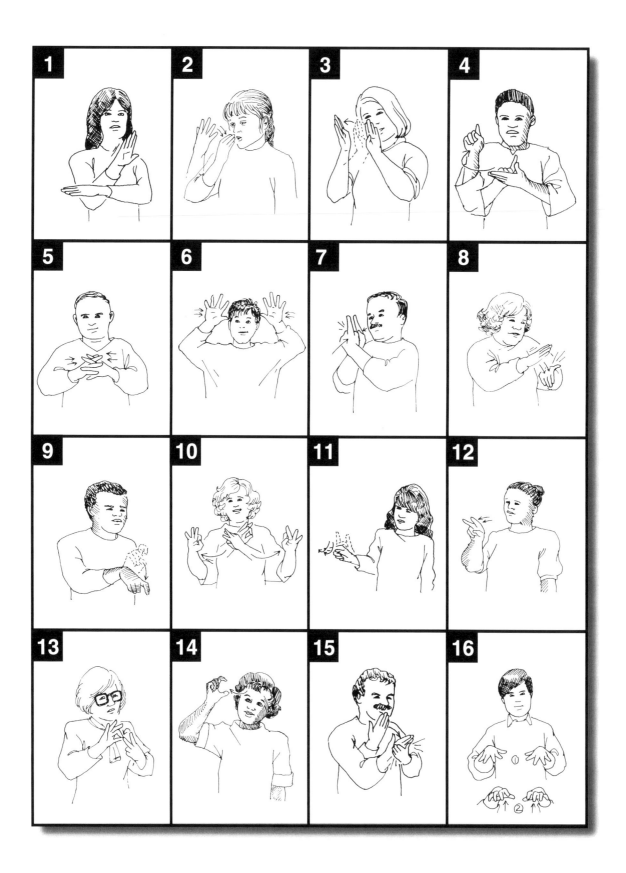

E13 Word Search

The gloss for each sign on the opposite page contains a double vowel, like "oo" in *soon*. Identify each sign and circle its gloss in the puzzle grid. The glosses are written horizontally, vertically, and diagonally. The letters may read forwards or backwards.

A	C	F	V	F	I	C	B	A	R	I	N	L
P	G	B	R	L	D	O	F	N	O	M	O	O
H	E	E	T	E	E	T	O	O	E	Y	O	P
K	E	T	J	G	E	H	O	H	E	E	M	F
D	S	G	I	R	A	C	T	I	K	E	R	O
J	U	C	N	E	E	K	B	Y	P	B	O	G
S	D	O	E	D	I	T	A	B	N	U	O	M
H	O	K	E	P	O	S	L	O	O	H	C	S
N	R	U	D	U	R	O	L	N	J	R	O	O
C	T	G	W	O	C	W	O	O	V	E	P	Y
E	B	O	O	P	O	H	N	F	O	E	V	S
E	N	O	L	G	E	B	O	L	V	K	I	M
Z	C	D	R	C	E	W	F	O	E	E	T	O
E	E	S	L	E	E	P	Y	M	S	R	O	O
E	H	E	E	R	A	Y	A	P	D	E	E	K
R	I	N	O	K	E	E	W	T	S	A	L	D
F	K	O	O	D	S	M	F	E	L	R	U	L
L	D	W	G	G	N	O	H	M	E	E	T	R

E14 Matching

All of the signs below are made with the 1 handshape. Match the glosses with their signs and write the letter or letters on the corresponding lines. Remember, a sign can have more than one English gloss.

A. ONE
B. WALKING
C. DOWNSTAIRS
D. LUST
E. COME HERE
F. THIRSTY

G. UPSTAIRS
H. THIRST
I. ALWAYS
J. DOWN
K. GO
L. SMART

M. COME
N. BLACK
O. WHERE
P. INTELLIGENT
Q. DEAF
R. UP

E15 Handshape Order

Identify the handshape used in each sign and write it on the line above the sign. Next, write the English gloss for each sign in the blanks below each illustration. Then, number the signs in the same order you would find them in *The American Sign Language Handshape Dictionary*. Write the numbers 1–14 in the circles. If you need help, look at the handshape chart on page 9, or in the dictionary. Remember, the one-hand signs come before the two-hand signs.

E16 Multiple-Meaning Crossword

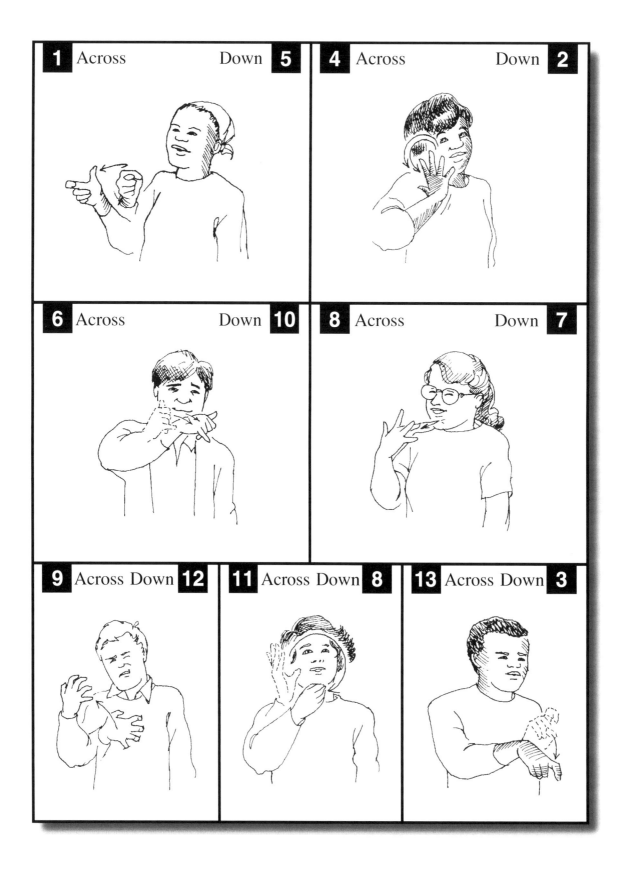

E16 Multiple-Meaning Crossword

A sign can be translated into more than one English word or phrase. Look at the signs on the opposite page; each sign has an "across" and a "down" answer. Write your answers in the spaces below. Good luck!

E17 Which One Doesn't Belong?

All but one gloss in each box represents a sign that begins with the movement written at the bottom of the box. Determine which gloss does not belong in each list and write the letter next to the gloss inside the circle.

1
- A. GOD
- B. NECKTIE
- C. LIVE
- D. QUIET

arc hand(s) down

2
- A. PURPLE
- B. SNOW
- C. PLAY-PIANO
- D. SPIDER

wiggle fingers

3
- A. BUG
- B. GRANDFATHER
- C. RABBIT
- D. STUBBORN

bend fingers

4
- A. PAIN
- B. NUMBER
- C. BORING
- D. WIND

twist hand(s)

5
- A. MOM
- B. DEER
- C. NEPHEW
- D. MAN

tap thumb(s)

6
- A. DIE
- B. INTO
- C. BET
- D. BECOME

flip hands over

7
- A. YES
- B. GUN
- C. COW
- D. UMBRELLA

bend wrist(s) down

8
- A. BLOND
- B. SALAD
- C. UP
- D. GROW-UP

move hand(s) up

9
- A. SHIP
- B. SEPARATE
- C. BACON
- D. WITHOUT

separate hands

10
- A. BOWL
- B. RAIN
- C. BASEBALL
- D. WONDERFUL

double bounce hands

11
- A. SHORT
- B. NAPKIN
- C. NOW
- D. CHILD

move hand(s) down

12
- A. HONOR
- B. REPLY
- C. SMILE
- D. LET

arc hand(s) forward

13
- A. ANGER
- B. BREAK
- C. GRAVE
- D. PEPPER

swing hand(s) up

14
- A. WHITE
- B. LIKE
- C. GAS
- D. PREGNANT

move hand(s) out

E18 Sign Descriptions

Each of the signs described below ends with the 5 handshape. Read the sign descriptions and make the signs. Then, write the English glosses on the lines at the end of each description. If you need help, turn the page to find the sign illustrations.

1. O > 5 • palm in, fingertips on chin • move hand out, opening to 5 handshape, palm up
    __ __ __ __

2. Flattened O > 5 • palm left, near head • bend hand down toward face while flicking fingers open twice __ __ __ __ __ __

3. 1 > 5 : 5 • right palm in, index finger on ear; left palm down, in neutral space • move right hand down, even with left hand, and shake both hands __ __ __ __ __ or __ __ __ __ __

4. S > 5 • palm down, neutral space • bend wrist down and flick fingers out __ __ __ __ or __ __ __ __ __ __   __ __ __

5. Open B > 5 : 5 • right palm in, in front of mouth; left palm up, in neutral space • brush hand up toward nose, then change to 5 handshape, palm down above left palm, and move hands in circular motion __ __ __ __ __ __ __ __ __

6. 1 > 5 • palm out, above head • draw a circle with index finger, then move hand toward head while opening to 5 handshape __ __ __ or __ __ __ __ __ __ __ __

7. Flattened O > 5 • palm left, at forehead • move hand down to chest while opening to 5 handshape __ __ __ or __ __ __ __ __ __ __ __ __

8. Bent 5 > 5 • palm in, fingertips on chin • brush fingers up and out, opening to 5 handshape __ __ __ __

9. Open 8 > 8 > 5 • palm in, middle finger and thumb on chest • move hand out, closing thumb and middle finger, then twist hand around and flick middle finger off thumb __ __ __ __   __ __ __ __

10. Flattened O > 5 • palm left, near head • drop hand down toward face while opening to 5 handshape __ __ __ __ or __ __ __ __ __

11. S > 5 • palm down, under chin • thrust hand out while flicking fingers out __ __ __ __ __ or __ __ __ __ __ __ __

12. S > 5 • palm up, in neutral space • shake hand slightly side to side, then throw it down, flicking fingers out __ __ __ __ __ __ __

Signs for E18

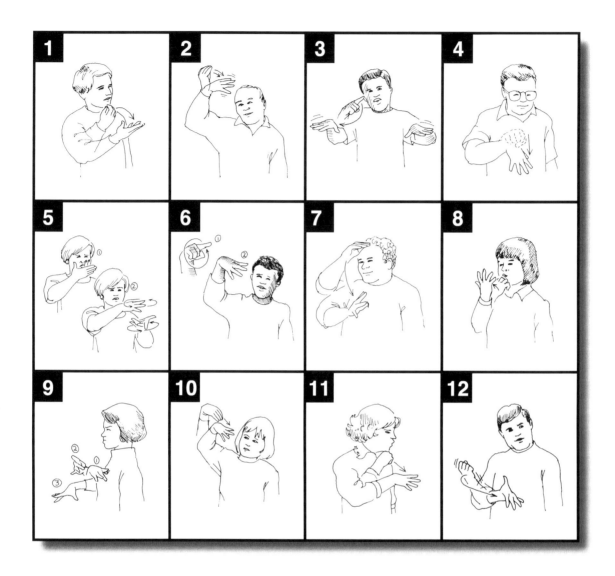

MEDIUM PUZZLES

M1 Crossword Puzzle

ACROSS

1	**3**
6	**7**
9	**11**
13	**15**
16	**17**

DOWN

1	**2**
4	**5**
8	**10**
11	**12**
14	**16**

M1 Crossword Puzzle

The signs on the opposite page are related to food. Look at each sign and write its English meaning in the spaces below.

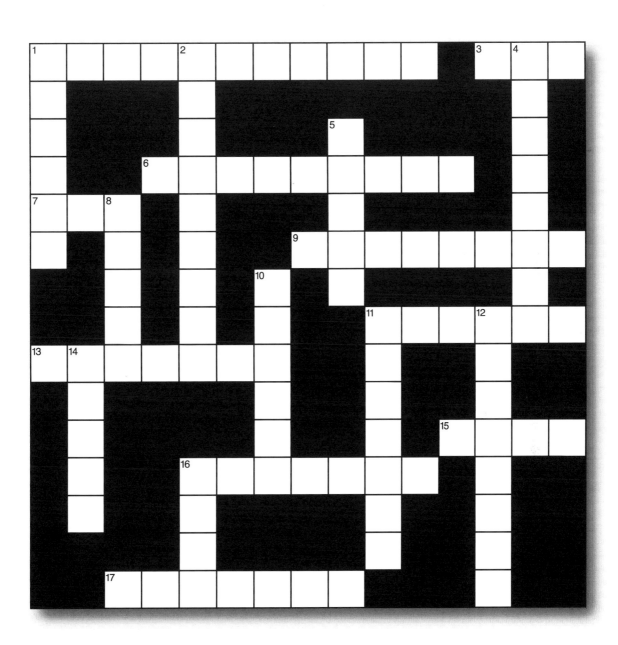

M2 Handshape Order

Identify the handshape used in each sign and write it on the line above the sign. Next, write the English gloss for each sign in the blanks below each illustration. Then, number the signs in the same order you would find them in *The American Sign Language Handshape Dictionary*. Write the numbers 1–14 in the circles. If you need help, look at the handshape chart on page 9, or in the dictionary. Remember, the one-hand signs come before the two-hand signs.

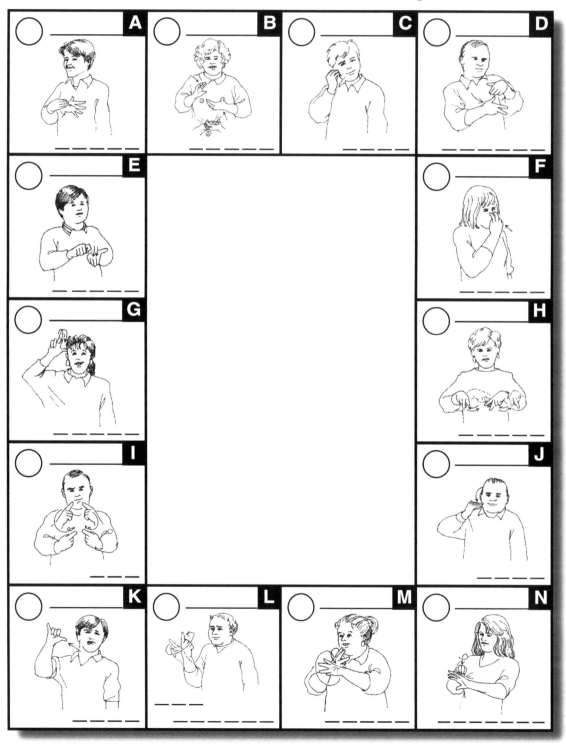

M3 Matching

All of the signs below begin at the mouth. Match the glosses with their signs and write the letter or letters on the corresponding lines. Remember, a sign can have more than one English gloss.

A. TOOTH
B. SMOKE
C. CHINA
D. KISS
E. QUIET
F. EVIL
G. FOOD

H. AM
I. RED
J. NAPKIN
K. BITE
L. DELICIOUS
M. THANKS
N. TELL

O. CALM
P. WICKED
Q. ICE-CREAM
R. THANK-YOU
S. BAD
T. EAT
U. SPIT

V. ARE
W. INNOCENT
X. BETTER
Y. LONELY
Z. BE
AA. TATTLE
BB. GLASS

M4 Multiple-Meaning Crossword

1 Across Down 4	3 Across Down 2	5 Across Down 11
7 Across Down 14	8 Across Down 12	9 Across Down 9
13 Across Down 16	15 Across Down 3	
17 Across Down 10	18 Across Down 6	

M4 Multiple-Meaning Crossword

A sign can be translated into more than one English word or phrase. Look at the signs on the opposite page; each sign has an "across" and a "down" answer. Write your answers in the spaces below. Good luck!

M5 Which One Doesn't Belong?

All but one gloss in each box represents a sign that is made at the location written at the bottom of the box. Determine which gloss does not belong in each list and write the letter next to the gloss inside the circle.

1
A. KID
B. ELEPHANT
C. STRICT
D. HAY
E. ALLERGY

near nose

2
A. GOD
B. TALL
C. LION
D. SUNSHINE
E. HEAVEN

above head

3
A. RIGHT
B. BURDEN
C. PAST
D. OUR
E. REAR

right shoulder

4
A. HEARING-AID
B. GOLD
C. LISTEN
D. EARRING
E. ALARM

ear or ears

5
A. TEASE
B. LETTER
C. FLAVOR
D. ORDER
E. EMBARRASS

lower lip

6
A. JEANS
B. WHEELCHAIR
C. JUMP
D. DOG
E. SLACKS

thigh area

7
A. DISAPPOINT
B. BAWL
C. WAKE-UP
D. WHAT-IF
E. SURPRISE

under eyes

8
A. COCA-COLA
B. HOSPITAL
C. SCOTLAND
D. SMELL
E. MONKEY

arm or armpit

9
A. BED
B. BROWN
C. CAKE
D. RUBBER
E. BLAME

cheek

10
A. WORRY
B. HAIR
C. BOSS
D. LETTUCE
E. WORSHIP

head

11
A. GLAD
B. FAT
C. BENEFIT
D. RABBI
E. YOUNG

chest

12
A. UNDERSTAND
B. NEPHEW
C. FUNERAL
D. THINK
E. PENNY

temple

13
A. GUITAR
B. RUSSIA
C. SHOW-OFF
D. FULL
E. ZIPPER

waist

14
A. CHOKE
B. POISON
C. HANG
D. STUCK
E. PENNILESS

neck

M6 Matching

All of the signs below can be associated with sports. Match the glosses with their signs and write the letter or letters on the corresponding lines. Remember, a sign can have more than one English gloss.

A. WRESTLING
B. KICK
C. BIKE
D. VICTORY
E. SCHEDULE
F. CAR
G. LUCKY

H. CANOE
I. OLYMPICS
J. SKI
K. CHEER
L. SWEAT
M. HURT
N. RACE

O. PERSPIRE
P. HUNT
Q. SPORTS
R. LOCKER
S. DIVE
T. SOCCER
U. PRACTICE

V. TOURNAMENT
W. WIN
X. ICE-SKATE
Y. DRIVE
Z. SATURDAYS
AA. COMPETE
BB. BICYCLE

M7 Multiple-Meaning Crossword

M7 Multiple-Meaning Crossword

A sign can be translated into more than one English word or phrase. Look at the signs on the opposite page; each sign has an "across" and a "down" answer. Write your answers in the spaces below. Good luck!

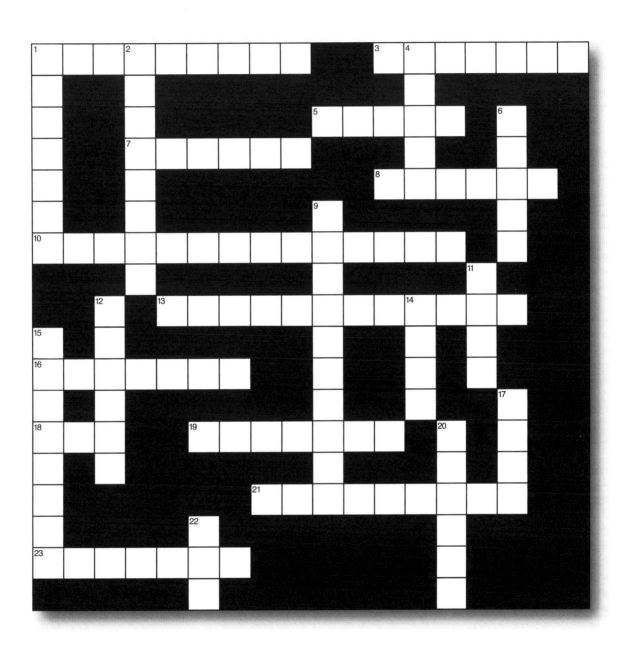

M8 Word Search

M8 Word Search

Each sign on the opposite page can be associated with school. Identify each sign and circle its gloss in the puzzle grid. The glosses are written horizontally, vertically, and diagonally. The letters may read forwards or backwards.

C	A	P	K	E	Y	H	F	P	R	S	U	M
H	D	R	O	P	O	U	T	D	A	J	E	L
E	F	M	Z	I	B	H	W	O	P	G	S	X
J	T	I	L	N	T	M	E	B	A	V	E	Z
G	U	A	N	S	W	E	R	U	Y	B	C	T
Q	K	C	U	Q	A	S	G	W	A	G	N	U
E	D	Y	H	D	R	N	I	N	T	J	E	P
B	S	Q	A	C	A	X	F	A	T	O	R	A
E	H	O	M	L	U	R	D	L	E	B	E	R
L	G	E	N	S	P	N	G	O	N	I	F	V
L	N	G	L	N	C	T	B	K	T	Z	N	A
R	I	Q	D	Y	W	H	E	V	I	Y	O	B
S	L	I	L	A	X	O	K	S	O	B	C	J
M	T	V	R	G	N	F	R	J	N	P	T	R
H	S	D	L	E	U	M	X	B	I	Q	U	Z
R	E	X	A	M	P	L	E	W	C	L	W	B
F	R	O	Q	D	Y	K	H	C	E	E	P	S
O	W	L	I	C	N	E	P	R	G	Z	N	P

M9 Crossword Puzzle

ACROSS

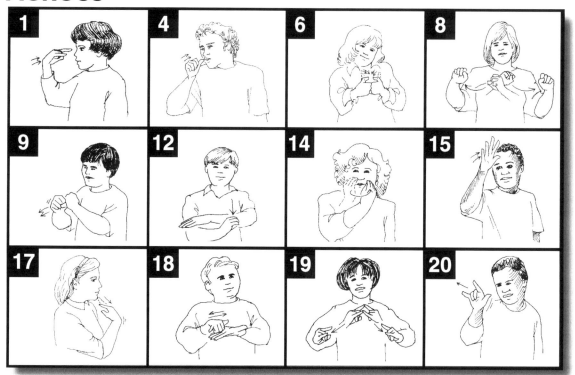

DOWN

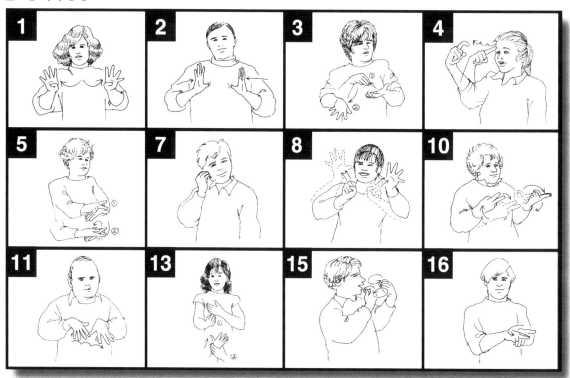

~56~

M9 Crossword Puzzle

Many of the signs on the opposite page are associated with holidays and celebrations. Look at each sign and write its English meaning in the spaces below.

M10 Word Search

M10 Word Search

The gloss for each sign on the opposite page has two sets of double letters, such as "dd" and "ss" in *address*. Identify each sign and circle its gloss in the puzzle grid. The glosses are written horizontally, vertically, and diagonally. The letters may read forwards or backwards.

E	S	D	U	R	B	B	A	F	F	G	S	Y
S	S	E	S	S	O	P	O	J	C	I	P	O
Y	C	E	V	A	P	O	B	S	S	K	E	N
A	L	W	I	C	T	T	M	A	T	L	E	C
D	L	L	M	B	T	O	V	M	M	U	C	A
D	E	F	A	H	J	P	O	J	A	F	H	N
N	E	L	I	N	N	F	A	P	T	T	L	P
O	L	A	V	K	O	R	R	I	G	E	E	W
I	G	C	O	W	H	I	J	N	I	N	S	R
S	S	O	L	A	K	E	T	U	N	A	S	J
S	Y	L	L	P	R	D	D	I	M	M	O	P
I	T	T	E	V	I	Y	L	L	D	U	C	E
M	I	D	Y	E	H	E	S	K	I	D	V	G
M	M	U	B	U	S	S	E	R	D	D	A	F
O	C	C	A	S	I	O	N	A	L	L	Y	E
C	O	V	L	O	B	O	I	W	R	U	O	L
L	I	L	L	N	E	S	S	E	R	P	P	O
U	Y	A	H	N	G	A	K	E	B	P	I	B

M11 Multiple-Meaning Crossword

MII Multiple-Meaning Crossword

A sign can be translated into more than one English word or phrase. Look at the signs on the opposite page; each sign has an "across" and a "down" answer.
Write your answers in the spaces below. Good luck!

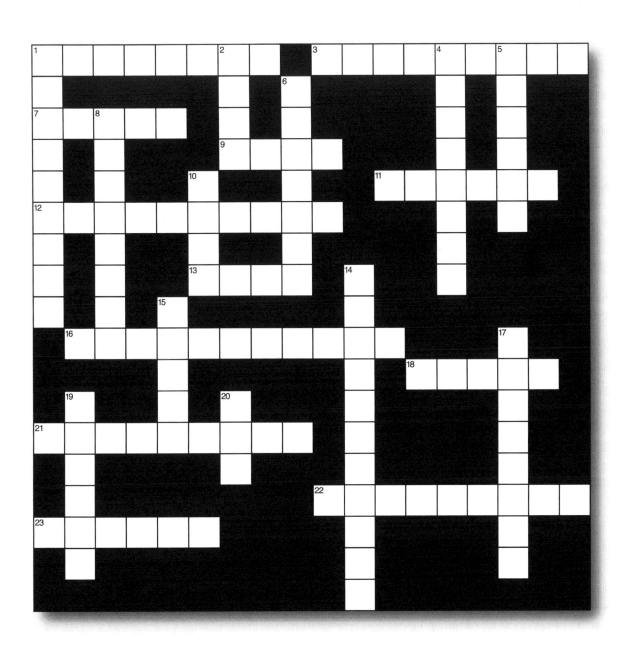

M12 Matching

All of the signs below have repeated movement. Match the glosses with their signs and write the letter or letters on the corresponding lines. Remember, a sign can have more than one English gloss.

A. HANG
B. WHY
C. LAND
D. MEDIUM
E. RADIO
F. WHAT?
G. WASH

H. COMPARE
I. FINE (texture)
J. WHAT'S-HAPPENING?
K. CLOSET
L. SCISSORS
M. LAUGH
N. TRAIN

O. AVERAGE
P. TOWEL
Q. CHAIN
R. YELLOW
S. DISTINGUISH
T. EARRING
U. SQUIRREL

V. GREEN
W. WHAT-ARE-YOU-DOING?
X. HANGER
Y. DRILL
Z. RAILROAD
AA. FLAG
BB. HAMMER

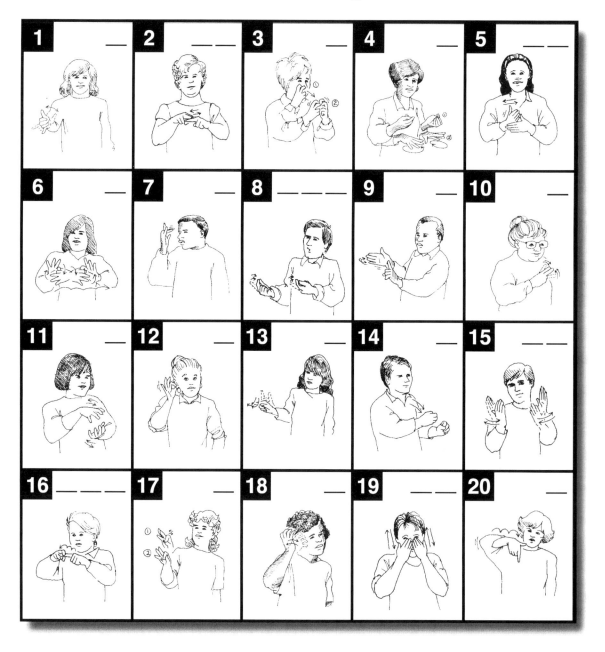

~62~

M13 Sign Descriptions

All of the signs described below represent feelings and emotions. Read the sign descriptions and make the signs. Then, write the English glosses on the lines at the end of each description. If you need help, turn the page to find the sign illustrations.

1. Baby O > 1 : Baby O > 1 • palms facing, under eyes • move hands out while flicking index fingers up __ __ __ __ __ __ __ __

2. Open B • palm out, near mouth • smack back of hand against mouth
   __ __ __ __ __ __ __ __ __

3. 5 : 5 • palms down, in neutral space • shake hands while moving them down
   __ __ __ __ __ __ __ or __ __ __ __ __ __ __

4. Bent 5 > S : Bent 5 > S • palms up, right hand slightly above left hand, in neutral space • move hands slightly down and out while closing to S handshape
   __ __ __ __ __ or __ __ __ __ __ __ __ __ __

5. Open B : Open B • palms together, in neutral space • rub hands back and forth several times __ __ __ __ __ __ __ __ __ or __ __ __ __ __

6. Bent 5 • palm in, near face • bring hand toward face in sharp, quick motion
   __ __ __ or __ __ __ __ __ or __ __ __ __ __

7. Open B : Open B • right palm left, index finger on lips; left palm down, in neutral space • pass right fingertips slowly under left hand __ __ __ __ __ __ __

8. 5 : 5 • palms in, in front of chest • move hands toward each other twice
   __ __ __ __ __ __ or __ __ __ __ __ __ __ __ __ __

9. Open B : Open B • palms in, right hand above left hand, on chest •
   __ __ __ __ __ __ or __ __ __ __ __ or __ __ __

10. 1 : 1 • right palm down, left palm right, in neutral space • bounce right index finger on middle of left index finger
    __ __ __ __ __ __ __ __ or __ __ __ __ __ __ __ __ __

11. Open B • palm in, on chest • move hand out a short distance __ __ __ __ __ __ __ __

12. 5 : 5 • palms in, right hand above left hand, in front of face • bring hands down in a sharp, short motion __ __ __ or __ __ __ __ __ __ __ __ __

Signs for M13

M14 Which One Doesn't Belong?

All but one gloss in each box represents a sign that begins with the palm or palms up. Determine which gloss does not belong in each list and write the letter next to the gloss inside the circle.

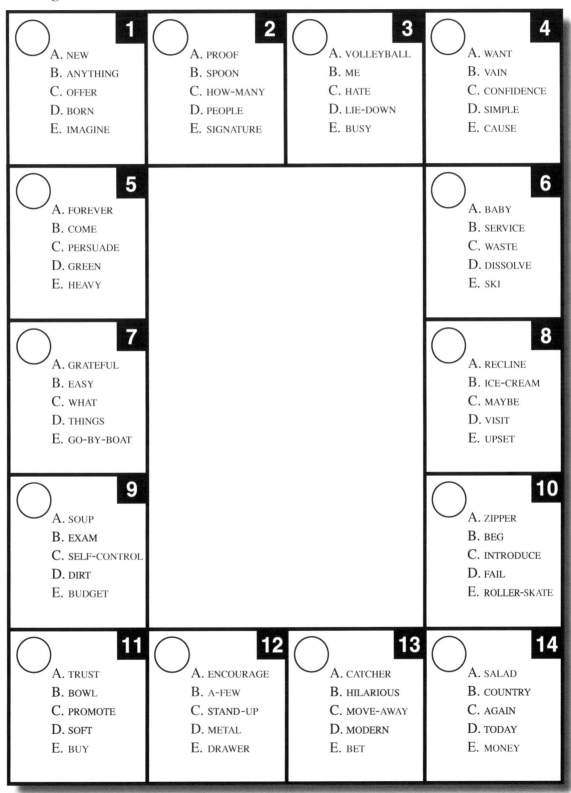

1
- A. NEW
- B. ANYTHING
- C. OFFER
- D. BORN
- E. IMAGINE

2
- A. PROOF
- B. SPOON
- C. HOW-MANY
- D. PEOPLE
- E. SIGNATURE

3
- A. VOLLEYBALL
- B. ME
- C. HATE
- D. LIE-DOWN
- E. BUSY

4
- A. WANT
- B. VAIN
- C. CONFIDENCE
- D. SIMPLE
- E. CAUSE

5
- A. FOREVER
- B. COME
- C. PERSUADE
- D. GREEN
- E. HEAVY

6
- A. BABY
- B. SERVICE
- C. WASTE
- D. DISSOLVE
- E. SKI

7
- A. GRATEFUL
- B. EASY
- C. WHAT
- D. THINGS
- E. GO-BY-BOAT

8
- A. RECLINE
- B. ICE-CREAM
- C. MAYBE
- D. VISIT
- E. UPSET

9
- A. SOUP
- B. EXAM
- C. SELF-CONTROL
- D. DIRT
- E. BUDGET

10
- A. ZIPPER
- B. BEG
- C. INTRODUCE
- D. FAIL
- E. ROLLER-SKATE

11
- A. TRUST
- B. BOWL
- C. PROMOTE
- D. SOFT
- E. BUY

12
- A. ENCOURAGE
- B. A-FEW
- C. STAND-UP
- D. METAL
- E. DRAWER

13
- A. CATCHER
- B. HILARIOUS
- C. MOVE-AWAY
- D. MODERN
- E. BET

14
- A. SALAD
- B. COUNTRY
- C. AGAIN
- D. TODAY
- E. MONEY

M15 Crossword Puzzle

ACROSS

DOWN

M15 Crossword Puzzle

All of the signs on the opposite page begin with the palms facing. Look at each sign and write its English meaning in the spaces below.

M16 Word Search

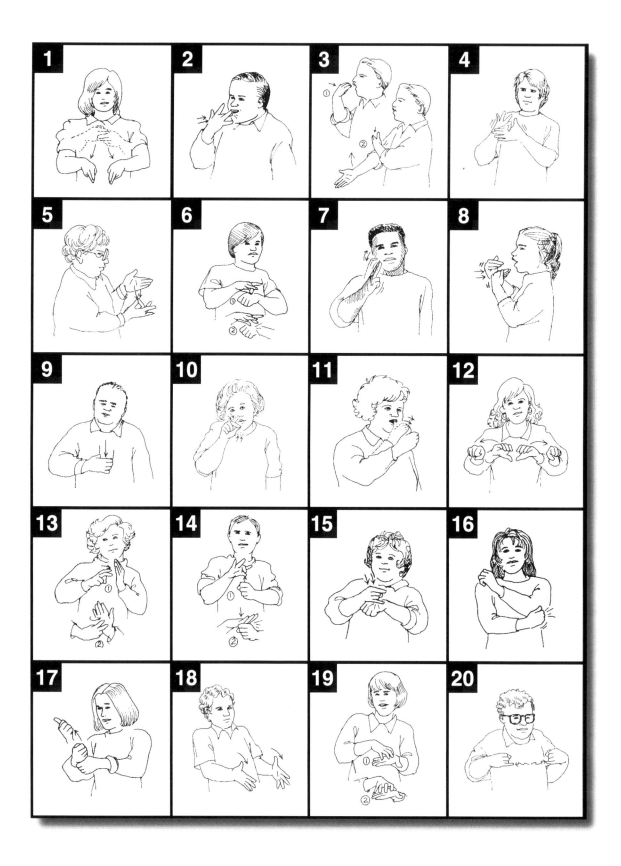

M16 Word Search

Each sign on the opposite page can be associated with food or eating. Identify each sign and circle its gloss in the puzzle grid. The glosses are written horizontally, vertically, and diagonally. The letters may read forwards or backwards.

E	G	L	F	U	I	C	S	J	U	D	N	E
B	G	S	A	N	D	W	I	C	H	F	I	G
N	E	K	C	I	H	C	H	Y	P	K	C	O
A	G	T	M	S	B	A	S	G	O	D	R	T
W	A	T	E	R	M	E	L	O	N	Y	A	F
H	R	O	O	P	R	K	C	Y	E	H	C	G
I	B	T	A	S	T	E	W	A	V	C	K	I
S	E	G	W	A	N	U	Y	I	M	A	E	D
K	N	U	B	O	V	C	T	R	F	T	R	N
E	G	M	A	R	O	T	H	E	I	V	O	G
Y	Y	K	P	R	E	G	L	V	H	A	J	W
K	B	R	E	H	B	A	G	O	D	T	O	H
A	T	M	G	I	S	P	K	T	O	H	T	E
E	F	A	J	N	B	I	M	F	N	R	S	B
T	P	E	A	N	U	T	P	E	A	K	A	F
S	J	G	D	H	R	H	V	L	E	S	O	K
R	U	L	T	C	V	M	E	N	C	A	T	C
M	D	E	P	O	P	A	D	O	S	L	P	H

M17 Matching

Each sign below can be associated with children or teenagers. Match the glosses with their signs and write the letter or letters on the corresponding lines. Remember, a sign can have more than one English gloss.

A. PICNIC	H. PIZZA	O. CLIMB	V. YELL
B. BEST-FRIEND	I. PERMISSION	P. SPORTS	W. RADIO
C. JOIN	J. LAUGHTER	Q. ENERGY	X. NAP
D. MAINSTREAM	K. BLANKET	R. OOPS	Y. PARTICIPATE
E. GO-STEADY	L. SCREAM	S. GOOD-FRIENDS	Z. LAUGH
F. PARTY	M. FALL-DOWN	T. DANCE	AA. COMPETE
G. RIVALRY	N. TIME-OUT	U. SANDWICH	BB. SHOUT

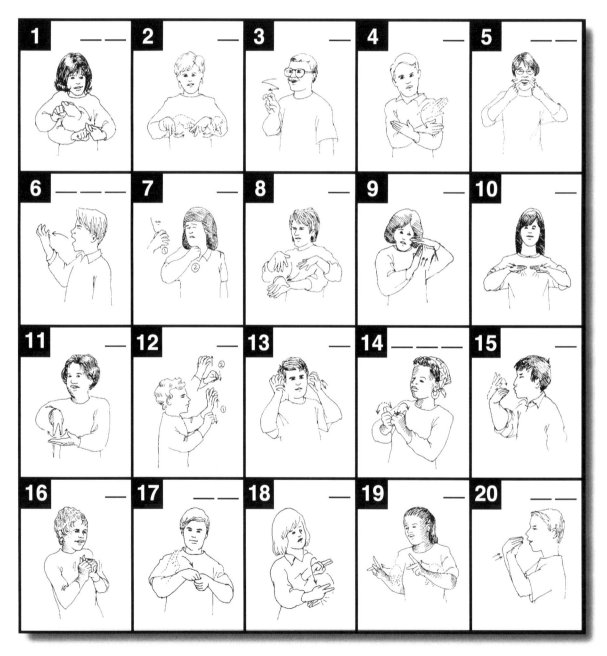

M18 Sign Descriptions

Each of the signs described below begins on the forehead. Read the sign descriptions and make the signs. Then, write the English glosses on the lines at the end of each description. If you need help, turn the page to find the sign illustrations.

1. I • palm in • move hand up and out __ __ __ __

2. 1 • palm left • swing hand out and around __ __ __

3. O • palm left • circle hand out from forehead twice __ __ __ __ __ __ __

4. Open B > Y • palm in • move hand forward and down while changing to Y handshape __ __ __

5. R • palm left • arc hand forward __ __ __ __ __ __ __

6. Open B • palm in, fingers up • flip hand out and down __ __ __ __   __ __ __ __ __

7. L > Bent L • palm in • wipe index finger across forehead to the right, then bend finger __ __ __ __ __ __ __

8. 1 • palm out • tap back of hand against center of forehead twice

    __ __ __ __ __ __ __

9. Open B > A • palm in • slide fingers across and off forehead, closing to A handshape __ __ __ __ __ __

10. Flattened O > 5 • palm left • move hand down to chest while opening to 5 handshape __ __ __

11. 1 > X • palm down • bend and straighten index finger several times while moving hand out __ __ __ __ __

12. H • palm left • arc hand forward __ __ __ __ __

Signs for M18

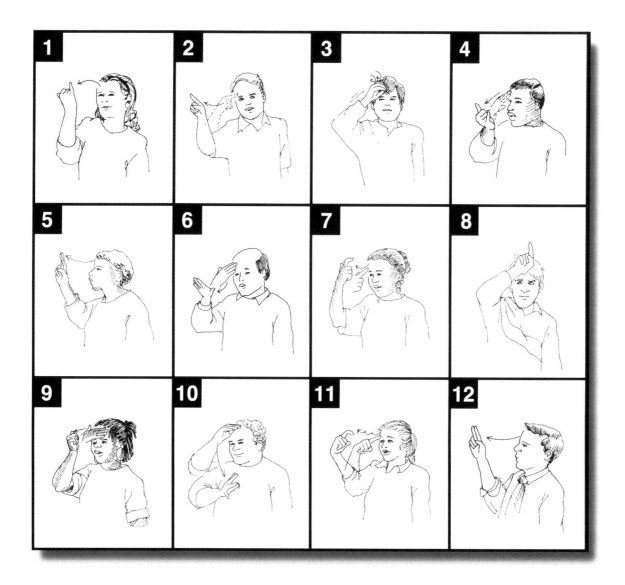

DIFFICULT PUZZLES

D1 Crossword Puzzle

ACROSS

DOWN

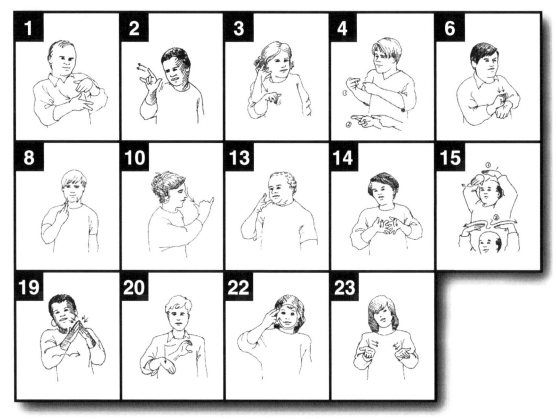

D1 Crossword Puzzle

The signs on the opposite page are for different places. Look at each sign and write its English meaning in the spaces below.

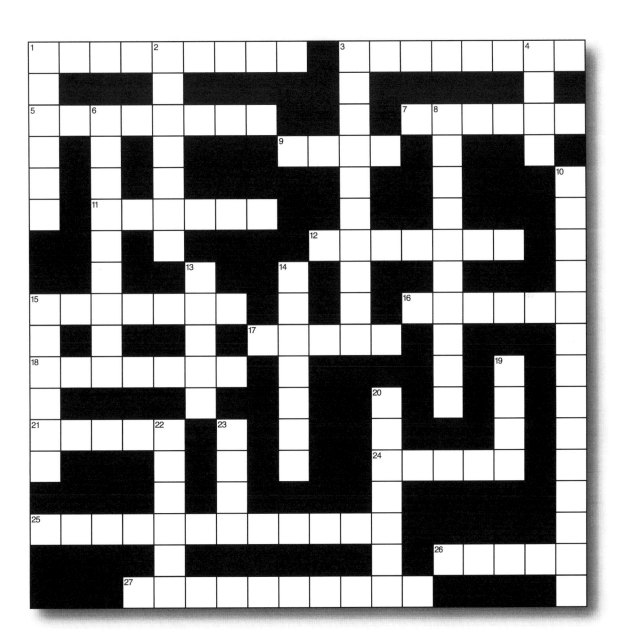

D2 Word Search

D2 Word Search

The gloss for each sign on the opposite page contains a double vowel, like "ee" in *feel*. Identify each sign and circle its gloss in the puzzle grid. The glosses are written horizontally, vertically, and diagonally. The letters may read forwards or backwards. This puzzle contains five extra glosses—see if you can find them all!

S	O	N	O	O	S	B	P	E	G	H	F	O
A	P	W	U	L	H	Y	D	E	E	R	G	P
K	E	E	P	T	E	K	O	N	E	I	R	D
M	E	C	E	W	E	E	O	E	S	M	O	O
G	B	J	L	C	P	N	L	E	H	O	K	O
D	O	O	F	I	H	A	F	M	W	O	O	R
O	O	L	M	C	K	R	V	A	F	R	J	B
H	T	O	O	L	A	T	E	T	I	C	E	E
B	E	E	O	E	G	Y	J	A	H	N	E	L
D	M	S	M	E	D	N	H	K	D	F	I	L
O	B	Y	O	F	R	C	P	W	Y	U	M	R
O	G	O	O	D	L	U	C	K	D	E	O	O
L	R	O	C	E	E	U	C	O	L	O	O	C
B	F	S	E	V	R	A	N	O	P	A	S	W
M	O	H	I	S	E	E	G	H	B	D	E	E
F	W	D	E	O	E	O	P	R	E	W	A	E
C	S	E	M	O	O	D	Y	L	E	E	E	P
V	K	B	A	P	E	E	L	S	R	E	V	O

D3 Crossword Puzzle

ACROSS

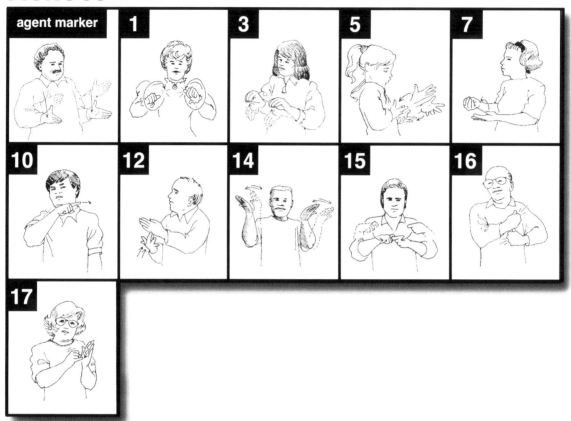

DOWN

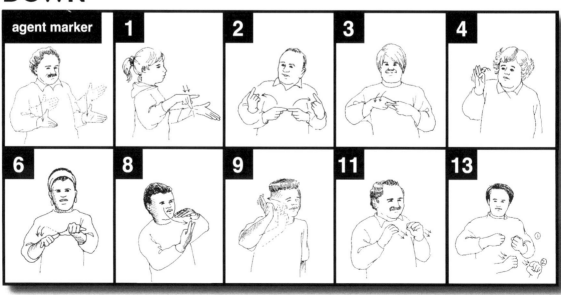

D3 Crossword Puzzle

When you add the agent marker to each of the signs on the opposite page, you create the sign for a person who performs the action depicted in the sign. For example, TEACH + agent marker = TEACHER. Look at each sign, add the agent marker, and write the resulting gloss in the spaces below.

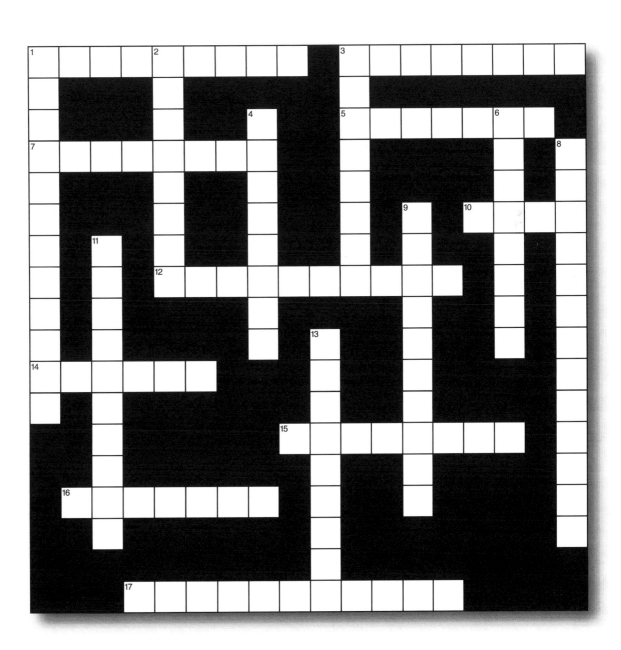

D4 Matching

All of the signs below begin with the palm or palms facing out. Match the glosses with their signs and write the letter or letters on the corresponding lines. Remember, a sign can have more than one English gloss.

A. PITY
B. BROWN
C. APPROXIMATELY
D. YES
E. SICK-YOU
F. CHANNEL
G. WEAR
H. REALLY
I. RUMOR

J. PERPLEXED
K. SITUATION
L. AROUND
M. SUPERINTENDENT
N. WANDER
O. YESTERDAY
P. COW
Q. PEST
R. ESTIMATE

S. PUZZLED
T. APPEAR
U. HEARING–AID
V. GOSSIP
W. MERCY
X. EAST
Y. USE
Z. PRESIDENT
AA. SYMPATHY

BB. SUNDAY
CC. UTILIZE
DD. KNOB
EE. COMPUTER
FF. HUH
GG. SEEM
HH. ROAM
II. NUISANCE

D5 Sign Descriptions

All of the signs described below begin with a C handshape. Read the sign descriptions and make the signs. Then, write the English glosses on the lines at the end of each description. If you need help, turn the page to find the sign illustrations.

1. palm in, fingertips on right side of chin • slide fingertips across to left side of chin

   _ _ _ _ _

2. palm left, right side of face • arc hand across face, closing to S handshape

   _ _ _ _ _   or   _ _ _ _ _ _   or   _ _ _ _ _ _ _ _   or   _ _ _ _ _

3. palms facing, left fingers on right fingers, in neutral space • slowly slide left fingers down right fingers, then slide right fingers down left fingers

   _ _ _ _ _ _ _ _ _ _

4. right palm out, thumb on left hand; left Open B, palm down; neutral space • close right fingers down on left hand _ _ _ _ _ _ _   or   _ _ _ _   _ _ _ _

5. palm left, near forehead • move hand back, ending with thumb on forehead

   _ _ _ _ _ _

6. palms out, right thumb on left 1 index finger, in neutral space • swing right hand around left index finger, ending palm in   _ _ _ _ _ _ _

7. palm in, fingertips on neck • shake hand slightly from side to side

   _ _ _ _ _   or   _ _ _

8. right palm in, hand on left palm; left Open B, palm up; neutral space• slide right hand off left hand, closing to S handshape

   _ _ _ _ _ _   or   _ _ _   _ _ _   or   _ _ _   _ _ _ _

9. right palm left, hand on left fingertips; left Open B, palm up; neutral space • slide right hand down left palm, ending palm in   _ _ _ _ _   or   _ _ _ _

10. palm in, fingertips on chest • rock hand up and down   _ _ _ _ _

11. palms facing, thumbs on chest • slide hands down to waist

    _ _ _ _ _ _   or   _ _ _ _ _ _ _ _   or   _ _ _ _ _ _ _

12. palms facing, hands around eyes • bend wrists twice   _ _ _ _ _ _ _ _ _ _

Signs for D5

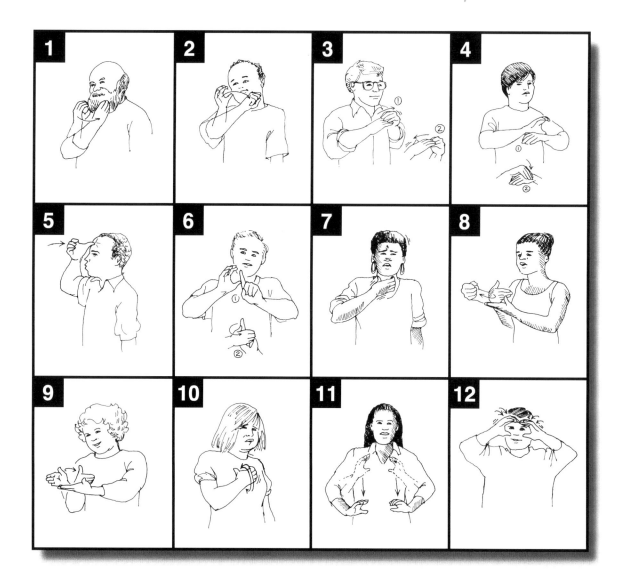

D6 Which One Doesn't Belong?

All but one gloss in each box represents a sign that has a circular movement. Determine which gloss does not belong in each list, and write the letter next to the gloss inside the circle.

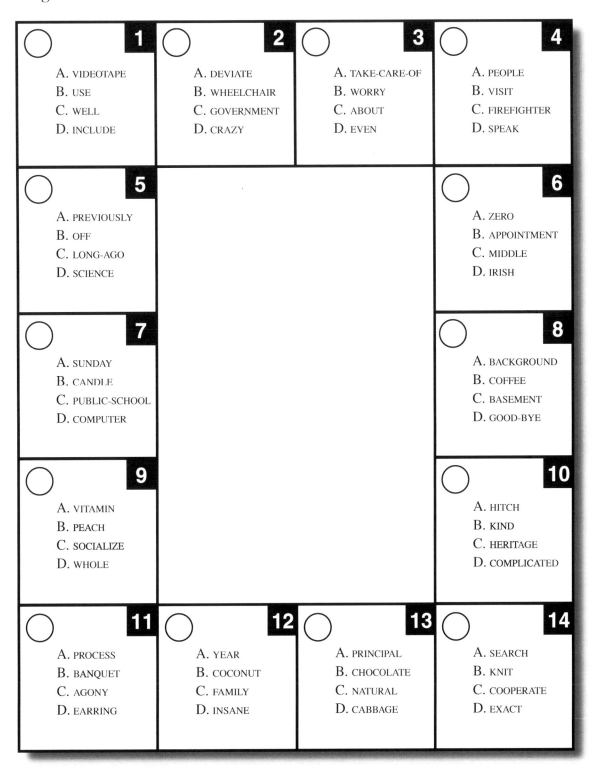

1

A. VIDEOTAPE
B. USE
C. WELL
D. INCLUDE

2

A. DEVIATE
B. WHEELCHAIR
C. GOVERNMENT
D. CRAZY

3

A. TAKE-CARE-OF
B. WORRY
C. ABOUT
D. EVEN

4

A. PEOPLE
B. VISIT
C. FIREFIGHTER
D. SPEAK

5

A. PREVIOUSLY
B. OFF
C. LONG-AGO
D. SCIENCE

6

A. ZERO
B. APPOINTMENT
C. MIDDLE
D. IRISH

7

A. SUNDAY
B. CANDLE
C. PUBLIC-SCHOOL
D. COMPUTER

8

A. BACKGROUND
B. COFFEE
C. BASEMENT
D. GOOD-BYE

9

A. VITAMIN
B. PEACH
C. SOCIALIZE
D. WHOLE

10

A. HITCH
B. KIND
C. HERITAGE
D. COMPLICATED

11

A. PROCESS
B. BANQUET
C. AGONY
D. EARRING

12

A. YEAR
B. COCONUT
C. FAMILY
D. INSANE

13

A. PRINCIPAL
B. CHOCOLATE
C. NATURAL
D. CABBAGE

14

A. SEARCH
B. KNIT
C. COOPERATE
D. EXACT

D7 Multiple-Meaning Crossword

D7 Multiple-Meaning Crossword

All of the signs on the opposite page are made with a double movement, and all of them can be translated into more than one English word or phrase. Look at each sign and write its meanings in the spaces below. Good luck!

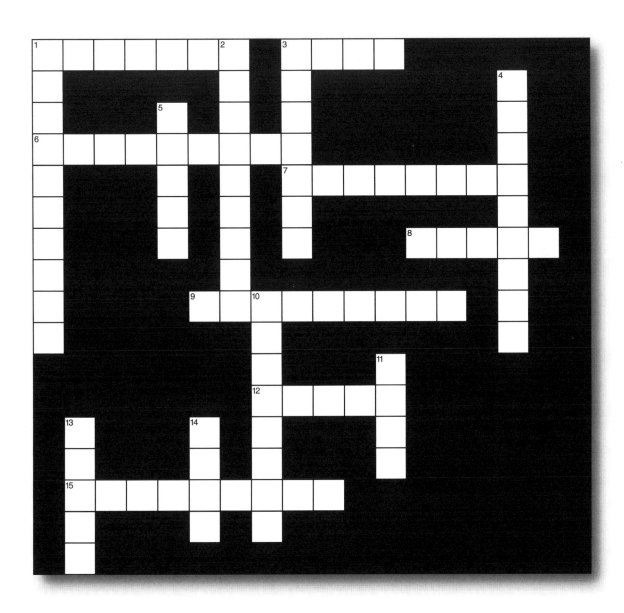

D8 Matching

Many of the signs below can incorporate the subject and object in the movement of the sign. Match the glosses with their signs and write the letter or letters on the corresponding lines. Remember, a sign can have more than one English gloss.

A. PAY
B. CONTRIBUTE
C. INFLUENCE
D. TAKE-ADVANTAGE
E. QUESTION
F. TEACH
G. DONATE
H. TAKE
I. ASK

J. SUPPLY
K. HELP
L. LEND
M. GIVE
N. SEND
O. ADVISE
P. NOTIFY
Q. CALL
R. KISS

S. FORCE
T. SHOW
U. SELECT
V. COERCE
W. ASSIST
X. GIVE
Y. INFORM
Z. INSTRUCT
AA. GIVE-YOU

BB. TELL
CC. CHOOSE
DD. BLAME
EE. MAIL-TO
FF. DEMONSTRATE
GG. PRESENT
HH. COUNSEL
II. QUIZ

D9 Sign Descriptions

How well can you recognize signs by their movement? Read the sign descriptions and make the signs. Then, write the English glosses on the lines at the end of each description. If you need help, turn the page to find the sign illustrations.

1. Tap left H hand twice with alternating right index and middle fingers __ __ __ __

2. Brush right thumb down cheek, then open hand and move arm down to rest on top of left arm __ __ __ __ __ __ __ __

3. Shake S hand slightly side to side, then throw hand down, flicking fingers out
   __ __ __ __ __ __

4. Tap top of head twice __ __ __

5. Tap right index finger on left palm, then reverse handshapes and repeat
   __ __ __ __ __ __

6. Slowly slide right fingers down back of left hand toward wrist __ __ __ __

7. Bounce right L hand, with index finger pointing down, while moving hand left
   __ __ __ __ __

8. Twist hands up and clasp hands __ __ __ __ __ __ __

9. Drop right H onto left H, then change both hands to C handshape and separate hands
   __ __ __ __ __

10. Move A hands down from mouth and out, changing to 5 handshape __ __ __ __ __

11. Sweep right thumb across fingertips from index finger to little finger
    __ __ __ __ __ __

12. Tap right index fingertip on left index fingertip, then rotate hands and repeat twice
    __ __ __ __ __ __ __ __

13. Bring right F hand down, brushing past left F thumb and index finger
    __ __ __ __ __

14. Move right Bent 3 hand toward left Open B hand, sandwiching edge of left hand between right index and middle fingers __ __ __ __ __ __

15. Hit middle of left Open B palm twice with right Open B fingertips
    __ __ __ __   __ __ __

16. Twist right 1 hand sharply up and forward __ __ __ __ __ __

Signs for D9

D10 Which One Doesn't Belong?

All but one gloss in each box represents a sign that is made in neutral space.
Determine which gloss does not belong in each list and write the letter next
to the gloss inside the circle.

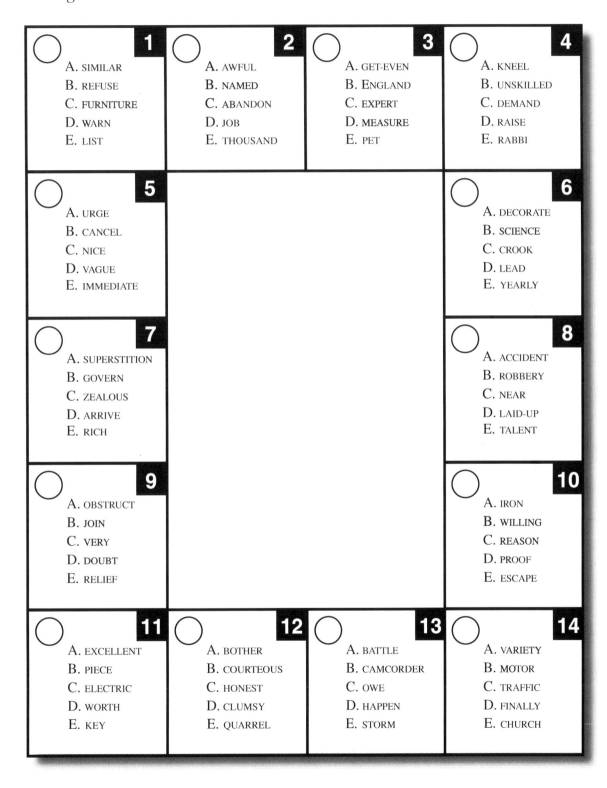

1
- A. SIMILAR
- B. REFUSE
- C. FURNITURE
- D. WARN
- E. LIST

2
- A. AWFUL
- B. NAMED
- C. ABANDON
- D. JOB
- E. THOUSAND

3
- A. GET-EVEN
- B. ENGLAND
- C. EXPERT
- D. MEASURE
- E. PET

4
- A. KNEEL
- B. UNSKILLED
- C. DEMAND
- D. RAISE
- E. RABBI

5
- A. URGE
- B. CANCEL
- C. NICE
- D. VAGUE
- E. IMMEDIATE

6
- A. DECORATE
- B. SCIENCE
- C. CROOK
- D. LEAD
- E. YEARLY

7
- A. SUPERSTITION
- B. GOVERN
- C. ZEALOUS
- D. ARRIVE
- E. RICH

8
- A. ACCIDENT
- B. ROBBERY
- C. NEAR
- D. LAID-UP
- E. TALENT

9
- A. OBSTRUCT
- B. JOIN
- C. VERY
- D. DOUBT
- E. RELIEF

10
- A. IRON
- B. WILLING
- C. REASON
- D. PROOF
- E. ESCAPE

11
- A. EXCELLENT
- B. PIECE
- C. ELECTRIC
- D. WORTH
- E. KEY

12
- A. BOTHER
- B. COURTEOUS
- C. HONEST
- D. CLUMSY
- E. QUARREL

13
- A. BATTLE
- B. CAMCORDER
- C. OWE
- D. HAPPEN
- E. STORM

14
- A. VARIETY
- B. MOTOR
- C. TRAFFIC
- D. FINALLY
- E. CHURCH

D11 Crossword Puzzle

ACROSS

DOWN

DII Crossword Puzzle

Many of the signs on the opposite page are associated with seasonal foods, clothing, or activities. Look at each sign and write its English meaning in the spaces below.

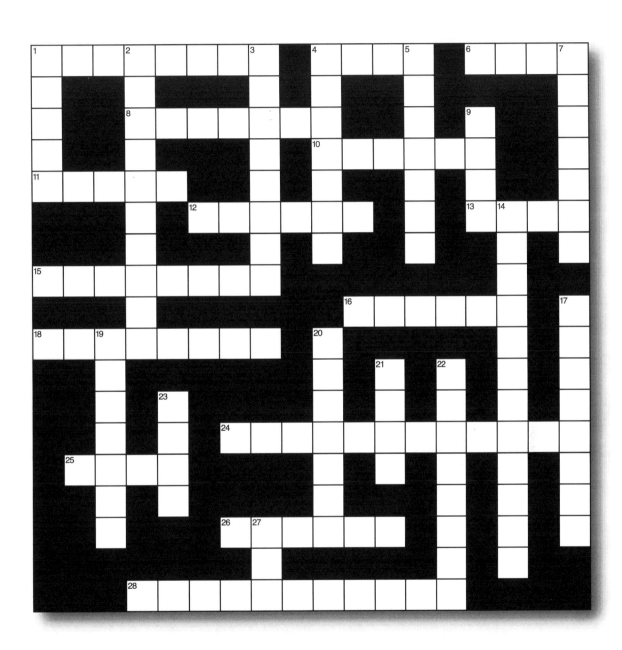

D12 Word Search

D12 Word Search

Many of the signs on the opposite page can be associated with sports. Identify each sign and circle its gloss in the puzzle grid. The glosses are written horizontally, vertically, and diagonally. The letters may read forwards or backwards. This puzzle contains five extra glosses—see if you can find them all!

N	O	I	T	A	L	U	G	E	R	G	P	W
D	T	S	A	Y	J	B	F	C	L	M	U	D
B	A	U	L	P	R	E	S	S	U	R	E	H
F	C	S	R	E	C	L	O	J	T	L	M	X
V	K	F	Q	N	P	L	Z	L	A	B	N	B
R	L	D	W	A	A	H	S	Y	E	N	O	M
E	E	S	O	L	Y	R	U	K	F	A	J	E
T	P	V	G	T	E	Q	O	M	T	T	B	D
A	S	O	N	Y	C	U	M	U	R	E	S	I
N	U	R	R	X	O	Q	A	Z	N	C	E	C
I	W	E	A	J	I	R	F	I	G	D	K	I
M	O	E	T	L	N	I	Z	E	A	H	P	N
I	N	D	U	R	U	A	D	I	V	P	F	E
L	K	G	Z	X	G	C	S	K	I	E	M	L
E	S	C	L	A	P	J	O	T	U	N	N	V
V	Y	D	M	O	B	P	U	N	C	H	I	T
R	F	R	A	C	T	U	R	E	I	W	E	O
H	Q	E	S	A	C	O	L	L	A	B	O	X

D13 Multiple-Meaning Crossword

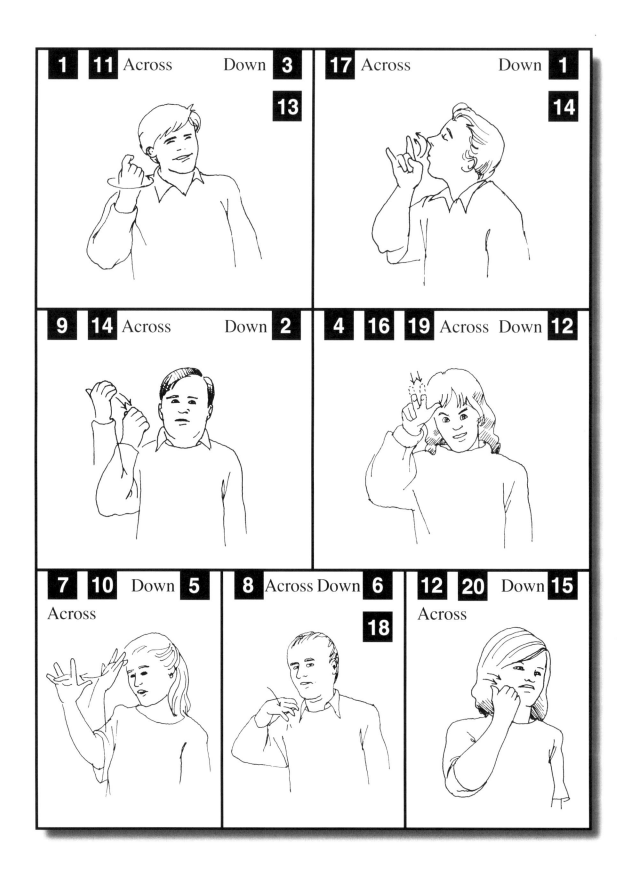

D13 Multiple-Meaning Crossword

All of the signs on the opposite page can be translated into more than one English word or phrase. Look at the each sign and write its meanings in the spaces below. Good luck!

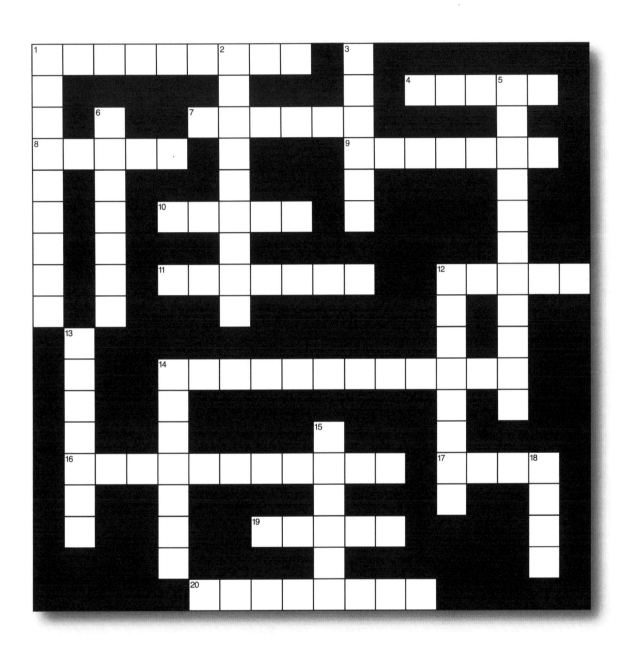

D14 Matching

All of the signs below are made by moving the hands down. Match the glosses with their signs and write the letter or letters on the corresponding lines. Remember, a sign can have more than one English gloss.

A. TUESDAYS
B. CAP
C. SUPPRESS-FEELINGS
D. STAY
E. PLATE
F. EVERY-TUESDAY
G. CURTAINS
H. OLD
I. SHORT

J. PRESENTLY
K. LORD
L. EVERY-MONDAY
M. PLATTER
N. SOUTH
O. TRADITION
P. SELF-CONTROL
Q. THANKSGIVING
R. NOW

S. LANDLORD
T. REMAIN
U. SMALL
V. KING
W. DRAPES
X. OBEY
Y. TODAY
Z. STILL
AA. CHILD

BB. NEVER
CC. TAN
DD. DISH
EE. AGE
FF. SARCASM
GG. MONDAYS
HH. HABIT
II. IRONIC

D15 Sign Descriptions

Read the sign descriptions and make the signs. Write the English glosses on the lines at the end of each description. If you need help, turn the page to find the sign illustrations.

1. 1 > C : C • bring right hand down from forehead and clasp hands together

    _ _ _ _ _ _ _

2. X : S • tap right fingertip on left wrist twice _ _ _ _

3. C > S > C > S : C > S > C > S • close and open hands twice while moving them apart _ _ _ _ _ _ _

4. Open B > Bent B • under chin • bend fingers down and up twice _ _ _

5. Bent L > A • move hand out from face and close hand _ _ _ _ _ _ _ _

6. V > H : C > S • slide right hand down left palm, closing fingers while left hand closes _ _ _ _

7. Bent L : L > Bent L • hook right index fingertip on left thumb and bend thumbs and left index finger while moving hands forward _ _ _

8. Open 8 > 5 : S • lift right middle finger out of left hand, then open hand and smack it down on top of left hand _ _ _ _   _ _ _

9. Open 8 > 8 > 5 • move hand out from chest, then twist hand around and flick middle finger off thumb _ _ _ _   _ _ _ _

10. Open N > Flattened O • close fingers and thumb sharply _ _

11. 1 > S : S • move right hand down from ear, closing hand, then move hands side to side in unison _ _ _ _

12. Open A > 3 • flip hand back on cheek while changing to 3 handshape

    _   _ _ _   _ _ _ _   _ _ _

13. G > L : G > L • open fingers up into L handshape _ _ _ _   _ _

14. 8 > Open 8 • flick middle finger up and off chin _ _ _ _ _

15. 1 : Open A • swing right index finger around to hit left thumb _ _ _ _ _

16. 5 : 3 • place right palm on left thumb and shake hand slightly as hands move forward

    _ _ _ _ _ _ _ _ _

Signs for D15

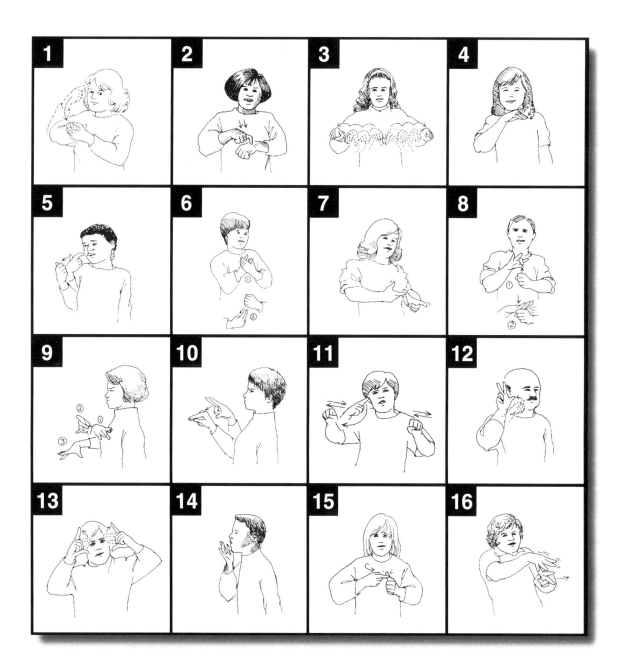

D16 Which One Doesn't Belong?

All but one gloss in each box represents a sign that ends in the handshape written at the bottom of the box. Determine which gloss does not belong in each list and write the letter next to the gloss inside the circle.

1	**2**	**3**	**4**
◯ A. EXPENSIVE B. DON'T-LIKE C. MAGIC D. FIREWORKS E. THROW-AWAY 5	◯ A. PENSION B. SPEND C. INTEREST D. STEAL E. NOT-GUILTY A	◯ A. DISTRIBUTE B. RUN C. IMMEDIATE D. POND E. REMOVE Bent L	◯ A. BIG-DEAL B. SHOOT C. TREASURE D. FASCINATE E. CRUEL S

5		**6**
◯ A. REFER B. OCEAN C. SOFT D. RECORD E. HILL Open B		◯ A. TRANSLITERATE B. SISTER C. WAKE-UP D. BROTHER E. LEAVE L

7		**8**
◯ A. GO-AWAY B. CAPSULE C. FOOTBALL D. AMENDMENT E. ABSENT Flattened O		◯ A. DEVIL B. CHANGE-THE-SUBJECT C. FROG D. ONE-HALF E. CHEWING-GUM V

9		**10**
◯ A. STATEMENT B. DISCOVER C. SELECT D. APPOINT E. GREASY F		◯ A. COUCH B. CONFERENCE C. BELIEVE D. HUSBAND E. ONE-HUNDRED C

11	**12**	**13**	**14**
◯ A. PIN B. ITALY C. TOO-LATE D. NARROW-MINDED E. LICENSE-PLATE Baby O	◯ A. DETACH B. EXPECT C. PIG D. PIE E. HYPOCRITE Bent B	◯ A. SPILL B. NOTHING C. BUSY D. SODA-POP E. DENY 5	◯ A. TATTLE B. COMPREHEND C. DIFFER D. DECIDE E. AMAZE 1

D17 Crossword Puzzle

ACROSS

DOWN

D17 Crossword Puzzle

All of the signs on the opposite page begin with the palms facing. Look at each sign and write its English meaning in the spaces below.

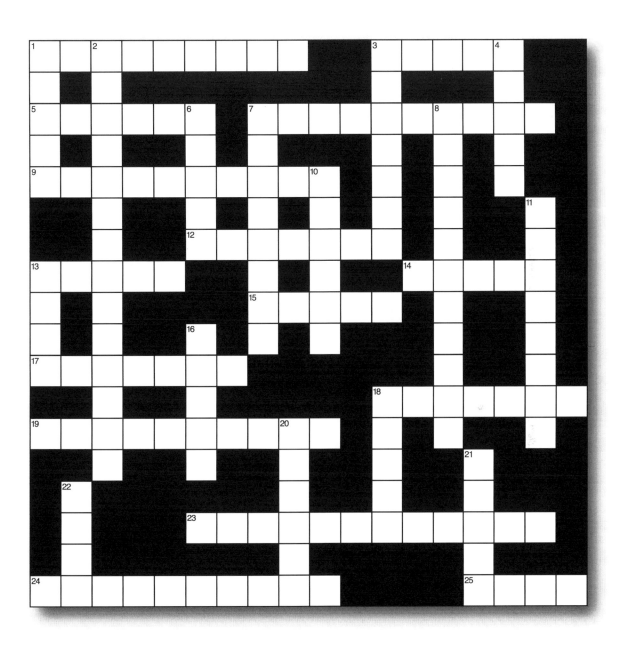

D18 Sentence-Building Puzzle

Write the English gloss for each sign inside its box. Then look at the English sentences below the signs and write the sentences again in ASL sentence order. Some of the signs will be used more than once.

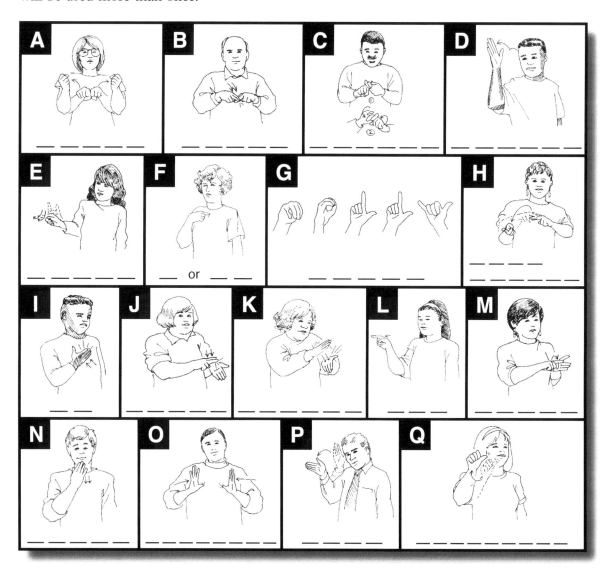

_____ _____

1. The chair is green.

_____ _____ _____ _____

2. My friend is a nurse.

_____ _____

3. Molly is sweet.

_____ _____ _____

4. In the future I will lose weight.

_____ _____ _____ _____

5. I broke the chair at school.

_____ _____ _____ _____

6. School vacation started yesterday.

ANSWERS

E1

B U T T E R F L Y   F R O G
- BEAR (down)
- ELEPHANT (down)
- FAITHFUL (down)
- STRAY (down)
- PROTECT
- INDEPENDENT (down)
- ANIMAL
- TURKEY
- SKUNK (down)
- CURIOUS (down)
- SNAKE
- ROOSTER
- RAT (down)
- ANTLERS

E2

#	Handshape	Letter	Word
14	Bent 5 : Bent 5	A	RAIN
9	Bent B : Bent B	B	HOW
6	4	C	TALK
3	Open N > N	D	DUCK
1	Open A	E	ANY
12	T : T	F	TRY
5	X	G	APPLE
7	Open 8	H	LUCKY
13	L-I : L-I	I	I-LOVE-YOU
8	A : A	J	GUITAR
11	L : L	K	BROTHER
4	S	L	SATURDAY
10	F : F	M	CAT
2	D	N	DINNER

E3

A. TIRED	G. YOUNG	M. KIND	
B. POLICE	H. LIKE	N. WE	
C. GRACIOUS	I. EXHAUSTED	O. BLOUSE	
D. INTERESTING	J. PRIDE	P. BREATHE	
E. EXHALE	K. COUGH	Q. US	
F. DRESS	L. GOWN	R. PROUD	

1. N Q
2. E P
3. A I
4. O
5. B
6. G
7. K
8. C M
9. J R
10. D
11. H
12. F L

E4

- PROPHET
- BUYER
- LUMBER (down)
- TEACHER (down)
- BARBER (down)
- ACTOR
- AUDIOLOGIST (down)
- WAITRESS
- ARTIST (down)
- STUDENT (down)
- SUPERVISOR
- PILOT

E5

E6

1. SUGAR
2. THIRSTY
3. WATER
4. FRUIT
5. ICE-CREAM
6. SALAD
7. BANANA
8. DRINK
9. GRAPES
10. HAMBURGER
11. POTATO
12. COFFEE
13. LUNCH
14. SALT
15. WINE
16. ORANGE

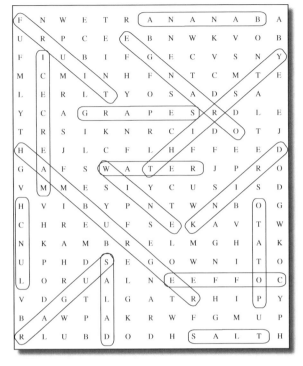

E7

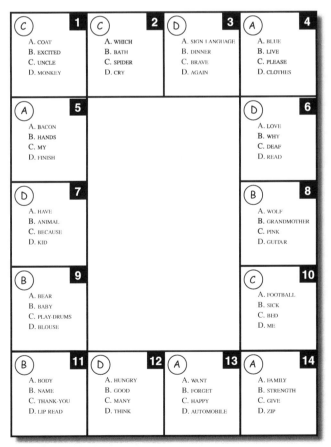

C **1**
A. COAT
B. EXCITED
C. UNCLE
D. MONKEY

C **2**
A. WHICH
B. BATH
C. SPIDER
D. CRY

D **3**
A. SIGN LANGUAGE
B. DINNER
C. BRAVE
D. AGAIN

A **4**
A. BLUE
B. LIVE
C. PLEASE
D. CLOTHES

A **5**
A. BACON
B. HANDS
C. MY
D. FINISH

D **6**
A. LOVE
B. WHY
C. DEAF
D. READ

D **7**
A. HAVE
B. ANIMAL
C. BECAUSE
D. KID

B **8**
A. WOLF
B. GRANDMOTHER
C. PINK
D. GUITAR

B **9**
A. BEAR
B. BABY
C. PLAY-DRUMS
D. BLOUSE

C **10**
A. FOOTBALL
B. SICK
C. BED
D. ME

B **11**
A. BODY
B. NAME
C. THANK-YOU
D. LIP READ

D **12**
A. HUNGRY
B. GOOD
C. MANY
D. THINK

A **13**
A. WANT
B. FORGET
C. HAPPY
D. AUTOMOBILE

A **14**
A. FAMILY
B. STRENGTH
C. GIVE
D. ZIP

E8

A. FUNNY
B. FASCINATE
C. LOUSY
D. SKUNK
E. DON'T-CARE
F. BUG
G. FOX
H. HUMOROUS
I. MEDDLE
J. RAT
K. COLD
L. PRY
M. NOSY
N. MOUSE
O. DON'T-MIND
P. FUN
Q. AMUSING
R. INSECT

E9

Crossword grid (E9) — solved:

- 1. SECRET
- WITCH (down)
- 2. VERYCLOSE
- COUNTEE (down)
- 3. SECOND (down)
- 4. TRADEPLACES
- 6. ENDORSE
- NEARBY (down)
- 7. PRIVATE (down)
- 8. APPRECIATE
- 9. PLEASE (down)
- 10. APPLY

E10

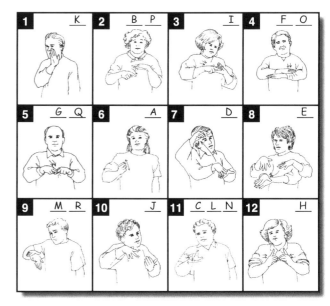

A.	HISTORY	G.	SIT	M.	TARDY
B.	ABSENT	H.	DATE	N.	FINGERSPELL
C.	SPELL	I.	CHEAT	O.	DESK
D.	LEARN	J.	STUDY	P.	SKIP-CLASS
E.	MAINSTREAM	K.	WHISPER	Q.	BE-SEATED
F.	TABLE	L.	ALPHABET	R.	LATE

Signs:
1 — K; 2 — B P; 3 — I; 4 — F O; 5 — G Q; 6 — A; 7 — D; 8 — E; 9 — M R; 10 — J; 11 — C L N; 12 — H

E11

1. E
A. BEARD
B. SUN
C. COMPUTER
D. COMPLAIN
E. CANADIAN
C

2. B
A. VOICE
B. BITE
C. SEE
D. STUCK
E. SMOKE
V

3. A
A. PLAY-CARDS
B. SALAD
C. BALL
D. SPIDER
E. AUDIENCE
Bent 5 : Bent 5

4. D
A. DEPRESSED
B. EXCITED
C. COMPUTER
D. DANGER
E. SICK
Open 8 : Open 8

5. C
A. RELAY
B. DOUGHNUT
C. RUNAWAY
D. ROOM
E. REPORT
R : R

6. C
A. LEFT
B. HAIR-DRYER
C. LIE
D. LUNCH
E. LAZY
L

7. B
A. LOUSY
B. BOY-SCOUT
C. VEHICLE
D. DEVIL
E. ROOSTER
3

8. E
A. WORSEN
B. ALL-NIGHT
C. TABLE
D. MUSIC
E. NOTHING
Open B : Passive

9. D
A. OLYMPICS
B. IMPORTANT
C. POSTPONE
D. FLEXIBLE
E. FAMILY
F : F

10. A
A. STRUGGLE
B. STRETCH
C. COLD
D. DEFEND
E. COFFEE
S : S

11. A
A. LIGHT
B. EAGLE
C. ONION
D. NEED
E. DETECTIVE
X

12. D
A. HANUKKAH
B. WAR
C. LINE-UP
D. TWINE
E. PRISON
4 : 4

13. C
A. ZERO
B. OPINION
C. WHO
D. NONE
E. PERCENT
O

14. B
A. ME
B. PRIVACY
C. RED
D. DEAF
E. ALWAYS
1

E12

Crossword grid (E12) — solved:

- 1. CRYOUT
- CHRISTMAS (down)
- 2. THURSDAY (down)
- 3. BITTER (down)
- SOUR (across)
- SHOT (down)
- 5. EVERYTHURSDAY
- 6. VALUE (down)
- 8. MOM / MOTHER (down)
- 9. SANTACLAUS
- 10. CHIN (down)
- 11. TREASURE
- 12. GLASS

E13

1. AFTERNOON
2. SLEEPY
3. DOOR
4. LAST-WEEK
5. FOOTBALL
6. DEER
7. MEET
8. SCHOOL
9. NEED
10. FREE
11. GREEN
12. LOOK
13. CHOOSE
14. MOON
15. GOOD
16. FREEZE

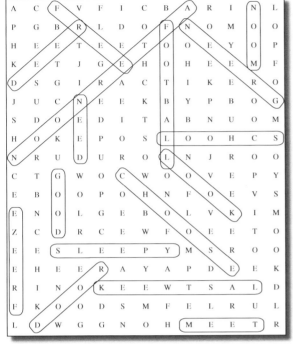

E14

A. ONE
B. WALKING
C. DOWNSTAIRS
D. LUST
E. COME HERE
F. THIRSTY
G. UPSTAIRS
H. THIRST
I. ALWAYS
J. DOWN
K. GO
L. SMART
M. COME
N. BLACK
O. WHERE
P. INTELLIGENT
Q. DEAF
R. UP

E15

E16

E17

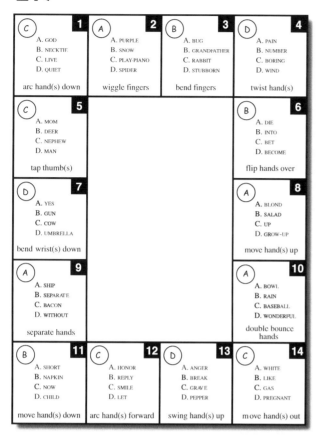

#	Circle	Options	Movement
1	C	A. GOD / B. NECKTIE / C. LIVE / D. QUIET	arc hand(s) down
2	A	A. PURPLE / B. SNOW / C. PLAY-PIANO / D. SPIDER	wiggle fingers
3	B	A. BUG / B. GRANDFATHER / C. RABBIT / D. STUBBORN	bend fingers
4	D	A. PAIN / B. NUMBER / C. BORING / D. WIND	twist hand(s)
5	C	A. MOM / B. DEER / C. NEPHEW / D. MAN	tap thumb(s)
6	B	A. DIE / B. INTO / C. BET / D. BECOME	flip hands over
7	D	A. YES / B. GUN / C. COW / D. UMBRELLA	bend wrist(s) down
8	A	A. BLOND / B. SALAD / C. UP / D. GROW-UP	move hand(s) up
9	A	A. SHIP / B. SEPARATE / C. BACON / D. WITHOUT	separate hands
10	A	A. BOWL / B. RAIN / C. BASEBALL / D. WONDERFUL	double bounce hands
11	B	A. SHORT / B. NAPKIN / C. NOW / D. CHILD	move hand(s) down
12	C	A. HONOR / B. REPLY / C. SMILE / D. LET	arc hand(s) forward
13	D	A. ANGER / B. BREAK / C. GRAVE / D. PEPPER	swing hand(s) up
14	C	A. WHITE / B. LIKE / C. GAS / D. PREGNANT	move hand(s) out

E18

1. WARM
2. SHOWER
3. NOISE or NOISY
4. DROP or FORGET IT
5. POLLUTION
6. SUN or SUNSHINE
7. MAN or GENTLEMAN
8. WARM
9. DON'T LIKE
10. LAMP or LIGHT
11. DENY or NOTHING
12. GAMBLE

M1

M2

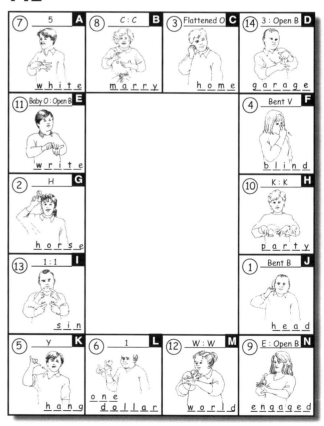

M3

A. TOOTH
B. SMOKE
C. CHINA
D. KISS
E. QUIET
F. EVIL
G. FOOD

H. AM
I. RED
J. NAPKIN
K. BITE
L. DELICIOUS
M. THANKS
N. TELL

O. CALM
P. WICKED
Q. ICE-CREAM
R. THANK-YOU
S. BAD
T. EAT
U. SPIT

V. ARE
W. INNOCENT
X. BETTER
Y. LONELY
Z. BE
AA. TATTLE
BB. GLASS

1 W	2 M R	3 X	4 L	5 Q
6 K	7 J	8 E O	9 I	10 G T
11 F P S	12 AA	13 A	14 C BB	15 N
16 U	17 H V Z	18 D	19 B	20 Y

M4

M5

1 D — A. KID / B. ELEPHANT / C. STRICT / D. HAY / E. ALLERGY — near nose	**2** B — A. GOD / B. TALL / C. LION / D. SUNSHINE / E. HEAVEN — above head	**3** A — A. RIGHT / B. BURDEN / C. PAST / D. OUR / E. REAR — right shoulder	**4** E — A. HEARING-AID / B. GOLD / C. LISTEN / D. EARRING / E. ALARM — ear or ears
5 A — A. TEASE / B. LETTER / C. FLAVOR / D. ORDER / E. EMBARRASS — lower lip			**6** C — A. JEANS / B. WHEELCHAIR / C. JUMP / D. DOG / E. SLACKS — thigh area
7 A — A. DISAPPOINT / B. BAWL / C. WAKE-UP / D. WHAT-IF / E. SURPRISE — under eyes			**8** D — A. COCA-COLA / B. HOSPITAL / C. SCOTLAND / D. SMELL / E. MONKEY — arm or armpit
9 E — A. BED / B. BROWN / C. CAKE / D. RUBBER / E. BLAME — cheek			**10** C — A. WORRY / B. HAIR / C. BOSS / D. LETTUCE / E. WORSHIP — head
11 B — A. GLAD / B. FAT / C. BENEFIT / D. RABBI / E. YOUNG — chest	**12** C — A. UNDERSTAND / B. NEPHEW / C. FUNERAL / D. THINK / E. PENNY — temple	**13** D — A. GUITAR / B. RUSSIA / C. SHOW-OFF / D. FULL / E. ZIPPER — waist	**14** B — A. CHOKE / B. POISON / C. HANG / D. STUCK / E. PENNILESS — neck

M6

A. WRESTLING
B. KICK
C. BIKE
D. VICTORY
E. SCHEDULE
F. CAR
G. LUCKY

H. CANOE
I. OLYMPICS
J. SKI
K. CHEER
L. SWEAT
M. HURT
N. RACE

O. PERSPIRE
P. HUNT
Q. SPORTS
R. LOCKER
S. DIVE
T. SOCCER
U. PRACTICE

V. TOURNAMENT
W. WIN
X. ICE-SKATE
Y. DRIVE
Z. SATURDAYS
AA. COMPETE
BB. BICYCLE

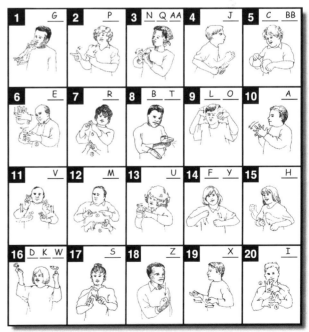

1 G	2 P	3 N Q AA	4 J	5 C BB
6 E	7 R	8 B T	9 L O	10 A
11 V	12 M	13 U	14 F Y	15 H
16 D K W	17 S	18 Z	19 X	20 I

M7

M8

1. HUH
2. SIGN LANGUAGE
3. DROP-OUT
4. RULER
5. WRESTLING
6. BOY
7. BROWNNOSE
8. ANSWER
9. PAY-ATTENTION
10. PENCIL
11. REBEL
12. PAGE
13. DRAW
14. SPEECH
15. GRADUATE
16. BELL
17. CONFERENCE
18. EXAMPLE
19. QUIZ
20. SUM

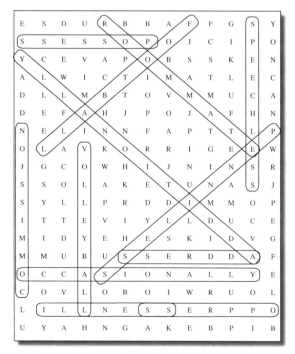

M9

M10

1. ROOMMATE
2. PENNILESS
3. OCCASIONALLY
4. ADDITIONALLY
5. FOOTBALL
6. COMMISSION
7. SPEECHLESS
8. VOLLEYBALL
9. ILLNESS
10. POSSESS
11. ADDRESS
12. OPPRESS

M11

Across/down answers visible in the grid: ALPHABET, ROUNDTRIP, DRINK, LAMP, WICKED, THOUGHTFUL, TAKE, INDIFFERENT, METOO, HEARTFELT, TOUCHING, APOLOGIZE, HOOKED, ADDICTION

M12

A. HANG
B. WHY
C. LAND
D. MEDIUM
E. RADIO
F. WHAT
G. WASH
H. COMPARE
I. FINE
J. WHAT'S-HAPPENING
K. CLOSET
L. SCISSORS
M. LAUGH
N. TRAIN
O. AVERAGE
P. TOWEL
Q. CHAIN
R. YELLOW
S. DISTINGUISH
T. EARRING
U. SQUIRREL
V. GREEN
W. WHAT-ARE-YOU-DOING?
X. HANGER
Y. DRILL
Z. RAILROAD
AA. FLAG
BB. HAMMER

No.	Answer
1	R
2	N Z
3	U
4	C
5	D O
6	Q
7	B
8	F J W
9	AA
10	L
11	M
12	T
13	V
14	BB
15	H S
16	A K X
17	I
18	E
19	G P
20	Y

M13

1. SURPRISE
2. FRUSTRATED
3. NERVOUS or ANXIOUS
4. TRUST or CONFIDENCE
5. AMBITIOUS or EAGER
6. MAD or ANGRY or CROSS
7. HUMBLE
8. AFRAID or FRIGHTENED
9. HAPPY or GLAD or JOY
10. POSITIVE or OPTIMISTIC
11. WILLING
12. SAD or DEJECTED

M14

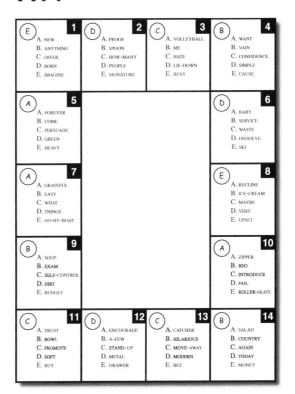

1 (E)
A. NEW
B. ANYTHING
C. OFFER
D. BORN
E. IMAGINE

2 (D)
A. PROOF
B. SPOON
C. HOW-MANY
D. PEOPLE
E. SIGNATURE

3 (C)
A. VOLLEYBALL
B. ME
C. HATE
D. LIE-DOWN
E. BUSY

4 (B)
A. WANT
B. VAIN
C. CONFIDENCE
D. SIMPLE
E. CAUSE

5 (A)
A. FOREVER
B. COME
C. PERSUADE
D. GREEN
E. HEAVY

6 (D)
A. BABY
B. SERVICE
C. WASTE
D. DISSOLVE
E. SKI

7 (A)
A. GRATEFUL
B. EASY
C. WHAT
D. THINGS
E. GO-BY-BOAT

8 (E)
A. RECLINE
B. ICE-CREAM
C. MAYBE
D. VISIT
E. UPSET

9 (B)
A. SOUP
B. EXAM
C. SELF-CONTROL
D. DIRT
E. BUDGET

10 (A)
A. ZIPPER
B. BEG
C. INTRODUCE
D. FAIL
E. ROLLER-SKATE

11 (C)
A. TRUST
B. BOWL
C. PROMOTE
D. SOFT
E. BUY

12 (D)
A. ENCOURAGE
B. A-FEW
C. STAND-UP
D. METAL
E. DRAWER

13 (C)
A. CATCHER
B. HILARIOUS
C. MOVE-AWAY
D. MODERN
E. BET

14 (B)
A. SALAD
B. COUNTRY
C. AGAIN
D. TODAY
E. MONEY

M15

M16

1. EGG
2. TASTE
3. BREAKFAST
4. STEAK
5. GRAVY
6. WATERMELON
7. GUM
8. SANDWICH
9. HUNGRY
10. CHICKEN
11. PEANUT
12. HOT-DOG
13. TOAST
14. SODA-POP
15. WHISKEY
16. CRACKER
17. CHAMPAGNE
18. LEFTOVER
19. COOKIE
20. SPAGHETTI

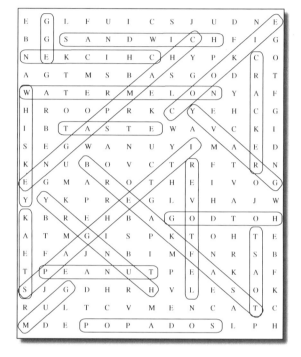

M17

A. PICNIC
B. BEST-FRIEND
C. JOIN
D. MAINSTREAM
E. GO-STEADY
F. PARTY
G. RIVALRY
H. PIZZA
I. PERMISSION
J. LAUGHTER
K. BLANKET
L. SCREAM
M. FALL-DOWN
N. TIME-OUT
O. CLIMB
P. SPORTS
Q. ENERGY
R. OOPS
S. FRIEND
T. DANCE
U. SANDWICH
V. YELL
W. RADIO
X. NAP
Y. PARTICIPATE
Z. LAUGH
AA. COMPETE
BB. SHOUT

M18

1. IDEA
2. FOR
3. OPINION
4. WHY
5. RESPECT
6. DON'T KNOW
7. BECAUSE
8. GERMANY
9. FORGET
10. MAN
11. DREAM
12. HONOR

D1

```
G A L L A U D E T ■ C E M E T E R Y
A ■ ■ I ■ ■ ■ ■ ■ ■ A ■ ■ ■ ■ ■ O
R E S T R O O M ■ ■ L ■ P R I S O N
A ■ Y ■ P ■ ■ ■ ■ ■ E ■ E ■ ■ ■ M
G ■ N ■ O ■ ■ J A I L ■ S ■ ■ ■ T
E ■ A ■ G ■ ■ ■ ■ ■ F ■ T ■ ■ ■ H
■ ■ G ■ A F R I C A ■ O ■ ■ ■ ■ E
■ ■ O ■ T ■ ■ ■ ■ ■ ■ N ■ ■ ■ ■ N
■ ■ ■ ■ ■ ■ ■ I R E L A N D ■ ■ E
■ ■ ■ ■ ■ R ■ F ■ ■ ■ T ■ ■ ■ ■ R
H I G H W A Y ■ A ■ ■ ■ B R I D G E
E ■ U ■ ■ U ■ O C E A N ■ ■ ■ ■ T
A M E R I C A ■ T ■ ■ C ■ ■ ■ C H
V ■ ■ ■ ■ ■ H ■ H ■ ■ N T ■ I ■ E
E A R T H ■ A ■ O ■ ■ ■ I T A L Y R
N ■ ■ ■ ■ ■ W ■ R ■ ■ ■ C ■ ■ ■ L
■ P H I L A D E L P H I A ■ ■ ■ A
■ ■ ■ ■ ■ ■ I ■ ■ ■ ■ ■ G W O R L D
■ ■ ■ H I G H S C H O O L ■ ■ ■ S
```

D2

1. OVERSLEEP	7. WHEEL CHAIR	13. BEER	19. BLOOD	EXTRAS:
2. FREE	8. TOO-LATE	14. SPEECH READ	20. FEEL	KEEP
3. GOOD-LUCK	9. ME-TOO	15. GREEDY	21. FLOOD	ROOM
4. SEEK	10. MOOSE	16. DOORBELL	22. SOON	WEEP
5. MOODY	11. WOOD	17. AGREE	23. OH-I-SEE	FOOD
6. POOR	12. FEE	18. COOL	24. SHEEP	HOOK

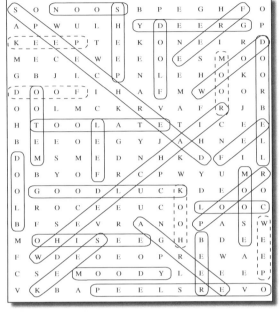

D3

D4

A. PITY	H. REALLY	O. YESTERDAY	V. GOSSIP	CC. UTILIZE
B. BROWN	I. RUMOR	P. COW	W. MERCY	DD. KNOB
C. APPROXIMATELY	J. PERPLEXED	Q. PEST	X. EAST	EE. COMPUTER
D. YES	K. SITUATION	R. ESTIMATE	Y. USE	FF. HUH
E. SICK-YOU	L. AROUND	S. PUZZLED	Z. PRESIDENT	GG. SEEM
F. CHANNEL	M. SUPERINTENDENT	T. APPEAR	AA. SYMPATHY	HH. ROAM
G. WEAR	N. WANDER	U. HEARING-AID	BB. SUNDAY	II. NUISANCE

~113~

D5

1. BEARD
2. GUESS or ASSUME or ESTIMATE or MISS
3. COMFORTABLE
4. DEFLATE or FLAT TIRE
5. GENIUS
6. CULTURE
7. CHOKE or GAG
8. EXPIRE or RUN OUT or ALL GONE
9. CREAM or SKIM
10. COUGH
11. CLIENT or CONSUMER or CUSTOMER
12. BINOCULARS

D6

1 (C)
A. VIDEOTAPE
B. USE
C. WELL
D. INCLUDE

2 (A)
A. DEVIATE
B. WHEELCHAIR
C. GOVERNMENT
D. CRAZY

3 (D)
A. TAKE-CARE-OF
B. WORRY
C. ABOUT
D. EVEN

4 (C)
A. PEOPLE
B. VISIT
C. FIREFIGHTER
D. SPEAK

5 (B)
A. PREVIOUSLY
B. OFF
C. LONG-AGO
D. SCIENCE

6 (A)
A. ZERO
B. APPOINTMENT
C. MIDDLE
D. IRISH

7 (B)
A. SUNDAY
B. CANDLE
C. PUBLIC-SCHOOL
D. COMPUTER

8 (D)
A. BACKGROUND
B. COFFEE
C. BASEMENT
D. GOOD-BYE

9 (A)
A. VITAMIN
B. PEACH
C. SOCIALIZE
D. WHOLE

10 (A)
A. HITCH
B. KIND
C. HERITAGE
D. COMPLICATED

11 (D)
A. PROCESS
B. BANQUET
C. AGONY
D. EARRING

12 (B)
A. YEAR
B. COCONUT
C. FAMILY
D. INSANE

13 (D)
A. PRINCIPAL
B. CHOCOLATE
C. NATURAL
D. CABBAGE

14 (B)
A. SEARCH
B. KNIT
C. COOPERATE
D. EXACT

D7

D8

A. PAY	I. ASK	S. FORCE	CC. CHOOSE
B. CON-TRIBUTE	J. SUPPLY	T. SHOW	DD. BLAME
C. INFLUENCE	K. HELP	U. SELECT	EE. MAIL-TO
D. TAKE-ADVANTAGE	L. LEND	V. COERCE	FF. DEMON-STRATE
E. QUESTION	M. GIVE	W. ASSIST	GG. PRESENT
F. TEACH	N. SEND	X. GIVE	HH. COUNSEL
G. DONATE	O. ADVISE	Y. INFORM	II. QUIZ
H. TAKE	P. NOTIFY	Z. INSTRUCT	
	Q. CALL	AA. GIVE-YOU	
	R. KISS	BB. TELL	

D9

1. SALT
2. DAUGHTER
3. GAMBLE
4. HAT
5. DEBATE
6. SLOW
7. DRILL
8. WEDDING
9. COUCH
10. BLESS
11. SEVERAL
12. RELATIVES
13. UNFAIR
14. TICKET
15. TIME OUT
16. INSULT

D10

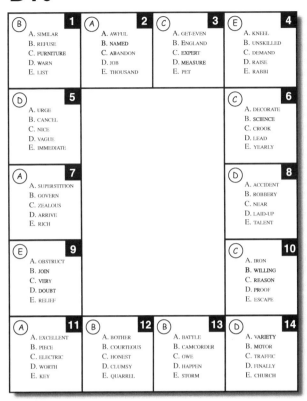

1 (B) A. SIMILAR / B. REFUSE / C. FURNITURE / D. WARN / E. LIST	**2** (A) A. AWFUL / **B. NAMED** / C. ABANDON / D. JOB / E. THOUSAND	**3** (C) A. GET-EVEN / B. ENGLAND / C. EXPERT / D. MEASURE / E. PET	**4** (E) A. KNEEL / B. UNSKILLED / C. DEMAND / D. RAISE / E. RABBI

5 (D) A. URGE / B. CANCEL / C. NICE / D. VAGUE / E. IMMEDIATE

6 (C) A. DECORATE / B. SCIENCE / C. CROOK / D. LEAD / E. YEARLY

7 (A) A. SUPERSTITION / B. GOVERN / C. ZEALOUS / D. ARRIVE / E. RICH

8 (D) A. ACCIDENT / B. ROBBERY / C. NEAR / D. LAID-UP / E. TALENT

9 (E) A. OBSTRUCT / B. JOIN / C. VERY / D. DOUBT / E. RELIEF

10 (C) A. IRON / **B. WILLING** / C. REASON / D. PROOF / E. ESCAPE

11 (A) A. EXCELLENT / B. PIECE / C. ELECTRIC / D. WORTH / E. KEY

12 (B) A. BOTHER / B. COURTEOUS / C. HONEST / D. CLUMSY / E. QUARREL

13 (B) A. BATTLE / B. CAMCORDER / C. OWE / D. HAPPEN / E. STORM

14 (D) A. VARIETY / B. MOTOR / C. TRAFFIC / D. FINALLY / E. CHURCH

D11

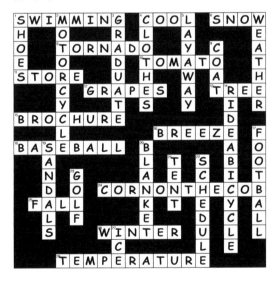

D12

1. PENALTY
2. EVENT
3. DEER
4. PUNCH
5. REGULA-TION
6. ELIMINATE
7. BOX
8. BINOCU-LARS
9. DELAY
10. TACKLE
11. COAX
12. PRESSURE
13. FRACTURE
14. TURN-AROUND
15. COIN
16. LOSE
17. BOAT
18. MEDICINE
19. RUN
20. MAGAZINE
21. BALL
22. FAST
23. BET
24. SKI

EXTRAS:
MONEY
FAMOUS
CLAP
JUMP
BELL

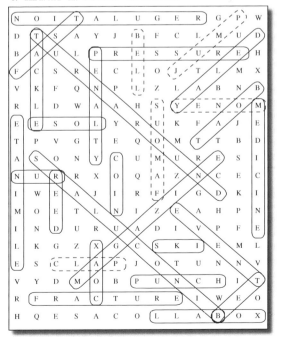

~115~

D13

```
C E L E B R A T E . . H . . . . .
O . C . . C L E V E R . U . D E V I L
C O A C H . O . . . R R O Y A L T Y
E . P . . W . . . A . . . . . E
I . T . S M A R T . Y . . . . L
T . A . . N . . . . . . . . . L
E . I . V I C T O R Y . . D A I L Y
D . N . . E . . . . . . D . . G
. T R I U M P H . S U B S C R I P T I O N
. . . . . . . . . T . . . E . . . . .
. M I S C H I E V O U S . S N O B
. . . . . . . . . M . . . H . . O
. . . . . . . D E M O N . . . . S
. . . . . . O R D I N A R Y . . S
```

D14

A. TUESDAYS
B. CAP
C. SUPPRESS-FEELINGS
D. STAY
E. PLATE
F. EVERY-TUESDAY
G. CURTAINS
H. OLD
I. SHORT
J. PRESENTLY
K. LORD
L. EVERY-MONDAY
M. PLATTER
N. SOUTH
O. TRADITION
P. SELF-CONTROL
Q. THANKS-GIVING
R. NOW
S. LANDLORD
T. REMAIN
U. SMALL
V. KING
W. DRAPES
X. OBEY
Y. TODAY
Z. STILL
AA. CHILD
BB. NEVER
CC. TAN
DD. DISH
EE. AGE
FF. SARCASM
GG. MONDAYS
HH. HABIT
II. IRONIC

#	Answer
1	K S
2	Q
3	D T Z
4	N
5	V
6	C P
7	L GG
8	BB
9	E M DD
10	FF II
11	B
12	H EE
13	I U
14	A F
15	X
16	J R Y
17	AA
18	G W
19	CC
20	O HH

D15

1. BELIEVE
2. TIME
3. SAUSAGE
4. PIG
5. INTEREST
6. BOTH
7. RUN
8. SODA POP
9. DON'T LIKE
10. NO
11. LOUD
12. A FEW DAYS AGO
13. WAKE UP
14. LIGHT
15. FIRST
16. HELICOPTER

D16

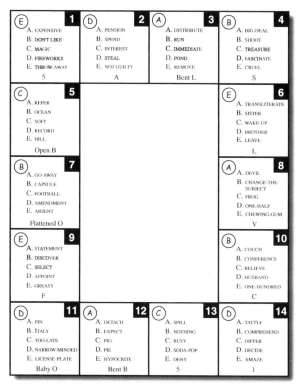

1 (E)
A. EXPENSIVE
B. DON'T LIKE
C. MAGIC
D. FIREWORKS
E. THROW-AWAY
5

2 (D)
A. PENSION
B. SPEND
C. INTEREST
D. STEAL
E. NOT-GUILTY
A

3 (A)
A. DISTRIBUTE
B. RUN
C. IMMEDIATE
D. POND
E. REMOVE
Bent L

4 (B)
A. BIG-DEAL
B. SHOOT
C. TREASURE
D. FASCINATE
E. CRUEL
S

5 (C)
A. REFER
B. OCEAN
C. SOFT
D. RECORD
E. HILL
Open B

6 (E)
A. TRANSLITERATE
B. SISTER
C. WAKE-UP
D. BROTHER
E. LEAVE
L

7 (B)
A. GO-AWAY
B. CAPSULE
C. FOOTBALL
D. AMENDMENT
E. ABSENT
Flattened O

8 (A)
A. DEVIL
B. CHANGE-THE-SUBJECT
C. FROG
D. ONE-HALF
E. CHEWING-GUM
V

9 (E)
A. STATEMENT
B. DISCOVER
C. SELECT
D. APPOINT
E. GREASY
F

10 (B)
A. COUCH
B. CONFERENCE
C. BELIEVE
D. HUSBAND
E. ONE-HUNDRED
C

11 (D)
A. PIN
B. ITALY
C. TOO-LATE
D. NARROW-MINDED
E. LICENSE-PLATE
Baby O

12 (A)
A. DETACH
B. EXPECT
C. PIG
D. PIE
E. HYPOCRITE
Bent B

13 (C)
A. SPILL
B. NOTHING
C. BUSY
D. SODA-POP
E. DENY
5

14 (D)
A. TATTLE
B. COMPREHEND
C. DIFFER
D. DECIDE
E. AMAZE
1

D17

D18

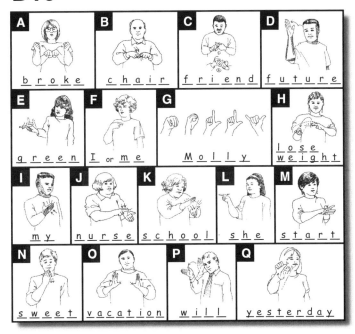

chair green
1. The chair is green.

my friend she nurse
2. My friend is a nurse.

Molly sweet
3. Molly is sweet.

future me lose weight
4. In the future I will lose weight.

chair school me broke
5. I broke the chair at school.

yesterday school vacation started
6. School vacation started yesterday.